manife
the internal revolu...

how to get
what you
want without
trying

BAREFOOT DOCTOR

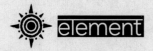 element

Element
An Imprint of HarperCollins*Publishers*
77–85 Fulham Palace Road
Hammersmith, London W6 8JB

The website address is:
www.thorsonselement.com

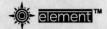

and *Element* are trademarks of
HarperCollins*Publishers* Limited

First published by Element 2004
This edition published by Element 2005

A catalogue record of this book
is available from the British Library

ISBN-13   978-0-00-732377-7

Mixed Sources
Product group from well-managed
forests and other controlled sources
www.fsc.org   Cert no. SW-COC-001806
© 1996 Forest Stewardship Council

FSC is a non-profit international organisation established to promote the
responsible management of the world's forests. Products carrying the FSC
label are independently certified to assure consumers that they come
from forests that are managed to meet the social, economic and
ecological needs of present and future generations.

Find out more about HarperCollins and the environment at
www.harpercollins.co.uk/green

Dedicated to the joyous memory of
Victor, Late Father of Barefoot

explanation of the scheme of the book

Hello, it's the author here with a short foreword I prepared earlier.

I've always entertained this strange fantasy of writing a book with no preamble whatsoever, as I see it as akin to running into the room before you've walked into the room and saying, 'In a second, I'm going to walk into the room and introduce myself and I just wanted to let you know beforehand, in case you got confused or upset in any way when I actually walk into the room.' I did try to do this this time, as I have done with all the books I've written – but as if my fingers had a mind of their own, they tapped away at the keys regardless until this preamble materialized. To be fair, the one that first appeared on screen was far shorter than this but when the Silver Shadow, my esteemed, fearsome and beloved ex-literary agent read it, she rounded on me with fury, declaring, 'Barefoot, you're always in such a rush to get started! I think this foreword needs more care and attention as it's the first thing people will see – you need to make clear from the start, for the sake of readers unfamiliar with your work, that you've already explained how to harness your power, how to meditate, become enlightened, spiritually aligned and even immortal in *Return of the*

Urban Warrior, and that you've explained how to free yourself from all self-limiting blocks to your perfect happiness in *Liberation*, and because you're not one to waste words, you don't intend to repeat yourself in this book – and that what you're about is high-speed transformation for people on the run, which is why *Manifesto* reads so fast it almost makes your eyes spin in their sockets ... and that it's also by far and away the very best self-help book you've ever written!'

But I reckon she said it for me, so I won't bother repeating it.

That all being said, after my customary semi-hypnotic introduction or, more accurately, induction, I launch unexpectedly, with a suddenness that surprised even me at the time of writing, into exactly what you do to manifest everything you always wanted, which takes up a good 58 per cent of the text (for those of you with a penchant for percentages). This comprises the slickest, most succinct and probably most powerful set of manifestation tools yet known to humankind and really should have had a far longer build-up, but I can't fake it with you – this material just isn't susceptible to showmanship, coming as it does from so far back in time and space.

You see, strangely, in spite of the fact that personally I am at least semi-certifiable, some ancient Taoist master or other, who evidently achieved spiritual immortality way back when, seems to have chosen me as his messenger. He probably had the wrong address, but that's fine with me, as I wasn't doing anything that special before all this started for me 38 years ago at the sweet, though not really innocent, age of eleven. And, after all, it's a great gig if you can get it. Of course, you could strip that version of events of its questionable romance and simply say it comes to me through the more rarefied channels of the higher mind, albeit filtered through decades of personal training, experience and distortion, direct, as it were, from source; from what you might call the Golden Immortals themselves, or at least from the Universal Dinner Lady (that'll make sense when you read the book).

The remaining 42 per cent (approximately) concerns itself with issues inevitably arising from the practice of manifesting things, as well as providing encouragement (because you'll be needing a fair bit of that) along with (hopefully) useful insights from the front line, arranged into short, easily downloadable chunks of data perfect for, say, a session on the loo or a couple of stops on the train on the way into or home from work. At first these drops of data may seem oddly repetitive but I'm sure you'll agree you can never have enough reminding of the basic metaphysical laws (I'm sure you'll agree).

It's quite feasible you could use at least 67 per cent or so of the text, if not far more, as an open-at-any-random-page style oracle or daily guidance mechanism with relative impunity and indeed gain quite some benefit. However, just because the actual how-you-do-it bit comes relatively early on in the text without massive fanfare, that doesn't mean you should skim through it, as this would have you missing the whole point, which after all, is learning how to get what you want the easy Taoist way. However, be warned (as will be repeated in the upcoming warning), that getting it can lead to significant personal disorientation, not to mention sometimes extreme upheaval in your social setting as regards sudden personnel or geographical changes and suchlike, as well as which your faith will be sorely tested many times over, hence why 33 per cent of information or thereabouts, addresses itself to helping you deal with that, or you could find yourself getting in a right old pickle, existentially speaking. That all being said, I hope you enjoy reading it 100 per cent, however you do it and whenever, and moreover I hope you enjoy the results, as without any shadow of a doubt, it's the best game I've ever played and I'm sure it will be for you too. (OK, will that do for you, Silver?)

warning

The method described and explained in this manifesto is extremely powerful and I'm not just saying that for dramatic or commercial effect. Furthermore, while it's true my style of delivery is variously jokey, lighthearted, compassionate, intimate, sexy, friendly, downright random and hopefully altogether enjoyable, don't let that fool you into thinking you're not playing with fire here.

Once you start using this manifesting method, your reality will begin to change and make you susceptible to occasional bouts of extreme disorientation, not just in your head but in your actual life. So don't mess about with this if you would really rather leave the conditions of your life as they are.

Remember, many people prefer wanting to actually getting and for good reason. We didn't create the suburbs and all that go with them – the mind-numbing TV, the drunken nights out, the Sunday shopping expeditions or the Friday night sex – for nothing. Real life can be very scary. Once you instigate the process of manifesting what you want, you have to leave the suburbs behind (and I use the concept of suburb figuratively) and step out into the big bad world where the wind of change blows with fury and there's nowhere to hide.

Obviously it's worth it because at the odd times the wind dies down, there's nothing as exhilarating as looking around you and saying, 'I manifested all this.' It's utterly magnificent in fact. But don't say I didn't warn you (and I'm not messing about when I say all this – trust me).

the internal revolution

Comrades, sisters and brothers of the world, the revolution has begun. No more confusion about getting what you want. The time has come to get what you want without confusion.

This is a bloodless revolution – but it's not for sissies. There will be disorientation. After aeons of confusion and clinging to the past, clarity is at first disorientating. This is only natural. Disorientation, however, is only disorientation and will pass as quickly as it came, leaving in its wake scenes of such splendour you will gasp in astonishment.

Have courage. This is a revolution of the heart. The heart will see things differently now and as it does, reality will change to match it. This may require you saying goodbye to many things of the past as the new makes itself known in your life. At times you will no longer recognize yourself as you struggle to grasp on to unfamiliar reference points.

be bold, for when the dust settles and the sound of galloping hooves fades into the distance, you will find yourself enjoying the life you always dreamed of but never really believed you could have.

Be bold, comrades, sisters and brothers, for when the dust settles and the sound of galloping hooves fades into the distance, you will find yourself enjoying the life you always dreamed of but never really believed you could have. And if you don't believe me either, read this manifesto and find out for yourself.

Not that I really mind – all faux-revolutionary propaganda aside – the internal revolution's already paid off for me, so I'm all right, Jack – but to increase my own good fortune, I know the only way is to share it. So I'm giving you the precise lowdown on exactly how it's done – the Taoist way – the way of *wu wei*, in fact – and you can use it or not as suits.

One thing's for sure, the more of us who do it now, the happier we'll all be, which will make me happier because I love it when people laugh and smile. It thrills me to the quick.

so, am I a jammy bastard?

I don't think so. I've worked patiently, consistently, tirelessly and lovingly for over twenty years, always faithful to the vision, never once wobbling in the face of constant obstruction and adversity, never complaining (except to one or two really close friends, who I actually drove half mad) about having no wealth or home for that time, never selling out and taking the conventional route to comfort, and doing it pretty much always with a smile and a cheerful heart. Yes, I'm a sensational guy; it's true. Sure, I have my faults, but then who doesn't. Sure, there are people who hate me and bless them all, but there are far more who love me and you know why, because I love you – you in everyone. It's as simple as that. And the you in everyone is the Tao, the Great Spirit, the Ineffable Suchness, generating, permeating, animating, connecting and informing the entirety of all creation, and if you love that, as I do, it loves you back, as you love me and I love you.

So no, not a jammy bastard at all, but a well-blessed bastard for sure, and damn thankful to life, myself and you that it's so. And now you can be one too – in fact you already are (you blessed bastard, you) – as I said, the revolution has begun whether you are aware of it or not.

But why bother? Why bother manifesting what you want – the Taoist way or any other way for that matter? Why rock the boat? Because unless you've learned to live your entire life in serene meditation without money, food, possessions or any other form of material sustenance ...

you've got to do something while you're hanging around waiting to die

Haven't you?

Well, possibly not. You could be a professional lotus-eater, hanging back in the cul-de-sac and never venturing another step on the Great Thoroughfare of Life. You could play safe, avoid the adventure, forget all about the revolution and mollify yourself with TV, banal conversation, second-rate sex, tainted romance and consumerism instead. You could, in other words, do nothing much and that would be fine – horses for courses, as it were. You could still read this manifesto – it would amuse you regardless.

But I tell you what, if you reckon on the fact that you're going to die anyway one day, and you never know exactly when that will be until it happens, and you figure from that that you've got nothing to lose and in fact everything in the entire world to gain, then with the data you access from reading this, you will, in no time, find yourself having a ball, baby, you'll find yourself having an absolute ball. So put on your dancing shoes and let's dance. Me, I go barefoot.

dancing with the Universal Dinner Lady
(or Universal Dinner Man, if you really want to be anal about it)

Manifesting the life you want is a dance you do with the Tao. That's the point of it. It is, to be crude about it, a spiritual experience. You see it's not the things, situations and events you manifest that bring you spiritual satisfaction, it's watching the Tao in action as those things, situations and events spring into existence before your very eyes – that's the blessing, that's the point (if there is one).

But what is this Tao you dance with? The Tao, the Great Spirit, the Ineffable Suchness, generating, permeating, animating, connecting and informing the entirety of all creation, is actually something you can't describe in words. It's simply far too big to fit within words no matter how well-configured or chosen, even for such a loquacious chap as I. But you can trigger the realization of it – after all, it's at the existential core of each and every one of us – by playing silly games. Traditionally, the Taoists of ancient times called it the mother of both existence and non-existence – note mother, not father. This alludes to its nurturing nature. But obviously the Tao is not really a woman, nor is it a man for that matter. This indicates that ancient

you've got nothing to lose
and in fact everything in the
entire world to gain.

Taoists were just as inclined to play silly games as post-modern ones, in which case come with me all the way into silliness here and picture this.

You're standing in line in the school canteen, Oliver Twist-style, your empty plate in your hands, shuffling along as kids do, looking down at the floor or at the dodgy haircut of the person in front of you. All of a sudden you find yourself at the front of the queue, and looking up you're startled and gratified to see that the dinner lady, far from the dowdy arche-type, is actually a voluptuous, sensuous, full-lipped, sex-goddess of a woman wearing silk underwear, suspenders, stockings and heels beneath her apron (or perhaps a firm-muscled sex-god, depending on your preference), who smiles at you bountifully and says, 'Yes? And what would you like, young woman (or man)?' Her body language, facial expression and vocal tone suggest you can ask for anything – anything in the whole wide world – and she'll heap it on your plate.

'I want everything,' you hear yourself say, 'not just purity or peace of mind, Dinner Lady, but absolutely everything.'

And rather than calling you a greedy little git, she smiles even more munificently than before and says, 'You got it kid, but dance with me first!' because she loves it when you ask for everything – it's her nature to give, to generate – it's what she's here for. And she loves a good dance. And that's why we love the Universal Dinner Lady so much.

As I said, it's silly, and I wouldn't want you, or me, to get stuck on it as a metaphor forever, but for now it's a good working proposition – not that a proper Taoist would indulge in such personifications, preferring the Tao to remain the formless, uncarved block of undiffer-entiated absoluteness it is. But for improper erstwhile Taoists like you or me, and for the sake of gaining some basic understanding of the nature of manifesting what you want, I suggest we indulge ourselves. And you know why? Because …

the Universal Dinner Lady
loves it when you ask for
everything – it's her nature
to give.

you create your own reality and can create it any old way you like

It's true. You can create a reality ruled by a scary ogre or one generated by someone as gorgeous and sexy as our beloved Universal Dinner Lady. It's all about models and which ones you use. All the great metaphysical systems and all the great religions are, when stripped of all superfluous dressing and emotion, merely models you've chosen, consciously or unconsciously, to adopt. Once adopted, models take on a power of their own, which then rule your life.

(A funny thought just struck me. Imagine a hundred years from now some well-meaning idiot finding this manuscript and starting a new religion based on worshipping our Universal Dinner Lady. By the altar stands the priestess or priest wearing a pinafore, silk underwear, stockings and suspenders, and dolloping mashed potatoes and mushy peas onto the plates of the devotees who come up for their weekly sacrament. I like it as an idea – it's got legs.)

But time is money and money is time, or so they say, so back to the plot. Your mind, when harnessed, is all-powerful and the way it describes reality to you is the way you'll believe it to be. Not only that – and here's the metaphysical twist that distinguishes this from a get-rich-quick book – the way you believe it to be is precisely the way it will play itself out on the stage of your world.

In other words, believe your world to be a hostile place where you have to fight for every scrap and morsel and that's the reality you'll have. You'll (unconsciously) transmit signals through body language, facial expression, vocal sound and sentence structure to everyone you meet, that say, 'Beat me, beat me!' Which is fine if you're into that sort of thing and you like suffering.

However, if you don't like suffering unnecessarily and want to enjoy yourself while you're on the planet, you're perfectly at liberty to believe your world a friendly, loving place where you need but ask and you will receive. And it will be so. It's really as simple as that.

There are actually no rules save the ones you make up. No restrictions other than the ones you invent. The world conforms to the beliefs you hold about it.

the world

The world is a concept. What do you mean by 'the world' when you say it? Whatever it is, you can be sure it's different, subtly or grossly, from what anyone believe your world to be a hostile place where you have to fight for every scrap and morsel and that's the reality you'll have.

else means when they say it. Yes, there will be common reference points – the planet's more or less round and it hurts when you bang your head, for example – we all agree on that – but beyond the basics, everyone's walking around with an entirely different concept of reality. Indeed, that's the fun of being here. We've tried it the other way – the way of forcing everyone to believe the same concept, but the history of divisions even in any single religion, not to mention divisions between the religions themselves, is proof enough that life doesn't work that way.

It's impossible to make people conform fully to an ideology because each of us, no matter how indoctrinated we are, invents our own reality. And as I say, that's the beauty of being here – the sharing of different ideas, views and gifts – it's what makes 'the world' go round.

So there's no objective reality, no 'the world' from a single point of view, only subjective reality, each of us living in our own worlds and coming together to share them. Then it's all down to whether you play nicely or not. Whether you share your world with love or defend it with fear and hatred.

And you're free to change your concept of the world as often or as radically as you like. For the purposes of this manifesto, however, I propose – should you be everyone's walking around with an entirely different concept of reality. and you're free to change your concept of the world as often or as radically as you like.

in earnest about getting what you want – that we conceive things along the lines of the Taoist schema, as follows.

wu wei

Wu wei (pronounced woo way) describes the process of our Universal Dinner Lady putting the proverbial food on your plate as soon as she's had a good twirl on the floor with you. Literally, it means the art of causing things you want to manifest of themselves without straining in any way. This doesn't imply laziness at all – you'll still have to work your arse off – that's the dance, but hard work never killed anyone. What kills people is the strain.

In fact our Universal Dinner Lady won't want to dance with you at all if you're straining in the Great Ballroom of Life – she'll find herself a more relaxed, gracious and nimble-footed partner until you've learned to ease off a bit.

So the first step is to relax.

hard work never killed anyone. what kills people is the
strain.

relax

Do you know how to relax? Do you know where to start? The answer lies in your body. Relax your body and your mind relaxes on its own. This is not to suggest collapsing on the floor, though – this is about relaxing every nerve and sinew as you dance. To achieve this most effectively, pay attention to the following tension build-up points, for by mentally releasing the tension accrued at these points, the whole body, and hence the mind, will relax.

Relax your solar plexus – the upper abdominal area, that houses your diaphragm; the muscle that makes your lungs work. Because this is where you process your emotions, it tends to become stuck and rigid through the inevitable residual build-up of emotional toxins and unprocessed pain and trauma we all accrue, which in turn causes blocking in the breathing pattern. As breathing freely is the major key to relaxing, it pays to remain mindful at all times of keeping this area relaxed enough to feel the sun shining in it all the time, even on the darkest day – hence solar plexus.

We describe controlling, rigid people as anal or tight-arsed for this very reason. The fear of the messy, chaotic underbelly of life that leads a person to feel the compulsion to attempt to control reality, to batten

relax your body and your
mind relaxes on its own.

down the hatches, naturally causes the anal sphincter muscles to contract and remain in a permanent state of contraction. As well as being unhealthy for the bowels, because the tension is transmitted throughout the intestines and stomach, this also causes the entire pelvic region to grow rigid. When your hips are stiff it's impossible to dance well and Dinner Lady (or Dinner Man) will be leading you off the dancefloor in no time. So let go of the tension here and feel your hips relax; and as your hips relax, notice that release spread up through your belly and back and down your thighs all the way to your toes.

Relax the back of your neck. Being stiff in the back of the neck and shoulder girdle also arises from trying to control life with your brain, hence why we also describe controlling people as stiffnecked. When you allow the back of your neck to soften and lengthen, your whole shoulder girdle and upper back relaxes and the blood flows to your brain better, which brightens up your thoughts and increases the sharpness of sensory input through eyes, ears, nose and mouth.

Relax your face. Because your face is the part of you that literally faces the world most, it accrues tension without you noticing – all those smiles held for too long, all those frowns – and that tension uses up precious energy that should be flowing throughout your

relax your anal sphincter
muscles. rude to mention it
in polite company perhaps,
but important.

body instead. Just allow all the expression to dissolve from your features; allow yourself to look like a simpleton and you'll feel the tension drain from the brain, through your throat and down the front of your body.

Finally, relax your chest. One of the finest compliments you can pay someone is to call them open-hearted and full of love. Everyone loves people like that, no less so our Universal Dinner Lady. You may think open-heartedness is something you're either born with or not but that's not true. Open-heartedness simply comes from having a relaxed chest. Not only that, the reduced pressure on the blood vessels connected to the heart and lungs helps you live longer so you have more time to perfect your moves on the dancefloor and hence manifest more. So let go of the tension in your chest now and feel the release radiate down your arms into your hands to generally make you more dextrous and hence able to handle life more effectively.

Obviously doing it just this once, though a fine and beneficial experience, is not going to be that useful in the long-term. To gain any long-term benefit, long-term enough to get some serious dancing done, you will need to continue repeating the practice pretty much all the time from now on till you die, while you work, rest or play.

one of the finest compli-
ments you can pay
someone is to call them
open-hearted and full
of love. everyone loves
people like that.

... may or may not have noticed then was ...ow of awareness from solar plexus, down to the groin, up the back to the back of the neck, over the head to the face and down through the throat and chest. This route is known as the 'microcosmic orbit' or loop. Moving your mind round it in an upward direction along the spine, over the head and in a downward direction down the midline of the front of the body, which in turn causes your energy to move likewise, is one of the most powerful metaphysical tools at your disposal. It is this, in fact, that is ...

the internal revolution

If you go deep enough into meditation or altered mind-states and you know what to look out for, you'll notice, at the deepest level of your being, a flow of what the Taoists call 'prenatal energy' in constant motion up the back of your spine, over your head and down the midline of the front of your body. It is this flow that causes all the constituent parts of the self to hold together in a meaningful enough shape for you to recognize yourself as a discrete entity, from the most profound to the most superficial level of being. At the superficial end of the scale, all you need do to recognize yourself as an entity is to look in the mirror, but the force that holds you together in one piece in order that you may position yourself in front of the mirror in the first place is this 'prenatal energy'. Even when you drop your body and die, say the Taoists, it will still be this flow that will hold you together in spirit form enough to recognize yourself – though of course this may be merely conjecture and does it matter anyway? However, what does matter is the huge significance of this fundamental force, which when consciously joined with lends you the manifesting power of the golden immortals (gods).

As soon as you learn to join your consciousness with it, you can manifest anything you want with ease. It would be tempting to waffle on about it for pages but it will be far more useful, from both our points of view, to get you started doing it immediately and subsequently to explain how to use it specifically for manifesting what you want. That way you can see how it works for yourself and it ceases to be merely an intellectual consideration. So, if that's OK with you, seat yourself comfortably so your weight is fairly evenly distributed between both buttocks and your spinal column is pretty much perpendicular to the horizontal. Run a scan over the aforementioned relaxation trigger points, starting with your solar plexus, allowing your breathing to settle into a smooth, even pattern. Relax your anal sphincter muscles and pelvis, lengthen and release the back of your neck, relax your face, your throat and chest, and feel your limbs soften all the way to your fingers and toes.

Now, as you inhale, visualize, imagine; visualize yourself imagining; imagine yourself visualizing; or simply feel the breath float up your spine from between your legs, through the back of your neck and up to the crown of your head. Now exhale and feel the breath float back down the front through your face, throat, chest, solar plexus, lower abdomen and pubic bone, to end up between your legs, ready to rise up the spine again.

If at first you find it hard to get your mind round the loop in time with the breath, simply move your awareness slowly round the loop while breathing naturally. Remember, this is only a device to join your consciousness with the prenatal flow that is occuring anyway. You're not trying to instigate something that wasn't already there, but be patient, because it can take anything from three seconds to three decades before the conscious link-up occurs. Not that that matters, because as soon as you start actively circulating your awareness round the loop, your enhanced manifesting power is activated, the full effect and significance of which will be shortly explained. But first, a few (thousand) more words on the basics of visualization and what-have-you.

practise awareness of this
internal revolution all the
time now, while doing
whatever else you do.

Meantime, practise awareness of this internal revolution all the time now, while doing whatever else you do during the day and night, whether at work, rest or play, and you'll notice within days how your body, mind and spirit feel stronger already.

Now, before going any further along this path of getting what you want the *wu wei* way, it behoves me to ask you this question in order that you may ask it of yourself (of course) …

what on earth do you want?

It's a strange thing. You walk around all day, every day, with an internal dialogue running in your head – a more or less uninterrupted conversation with yourself about what you want – yet as soon as someone – maybe an angel, maybe a barefoot doctor – asks you what you want, you go, 'hmmm…' and get all confused as a thousand images whirl kaleidoscopically around your forebrain. So, to make it simple, allow me to humbly present the basic common denominators at the root of all human desire, not necessarily, but probably, in order of importance:

clean air
pure water
uncontaminated food
shelter
clothing (including for the
    sake of convenience,
    shoes, accessories and
    all hair, skin and bath
    products, perfumes,
    tweezers, nail clippers,
    razors and all the gubbins
    you need to make you
    feel presentable)
physical warmth
physical comfort
strength
stamina
energy
health
longevity
physical beauty
confidence
freedom of movement
    (including viable
    transportation
    methods)
sex
empathetic company
    (human warmth)
freedom of ideas

freedom of choice
freedom of expression
love
respect
gainful, fulfilling
    employment
social status
a good reputation
popularity (maybe
    involving fame)
safety
entertainment
a feeling of belonging
    (wherever you are)
peace of mind (including
    being at peace with the
    idea of dying one day
    as well as having a
    workable, reliable
    philosophy or existential
    model that may or
    may not have spiritual
    underpinnings)
purity of heart (hence
    authenticity and
    intensity of experience)
lots and lots of fun,
    laughter and smiles
and, of course, loads and
    loads of money

And all of these go along with the underlying drive to continually improve the quality of each one once you have it, and usually to increase the quantity as well – more, more, more, in other words.

What do you reckon, have I left anything off the list? You'll probably shout, 'happiness!', but that's a stupid thing to try and manifest as happiness comes and goes of its own accord and trying to become attached to it when it comes only leads to disappointment when it goes. Hence why peace of mind is on the list instead, because that you can rely on, whether happy or not, which tends to make you generally rather happy anyway.

Throw it around any way you like, I think that pretty much covers it, though, one way or another. So shall we take that as the template for our manifesto of man-ifestation? The rest is all down to you embellishing it, colouring it and tailoring it to your own specifications. So what prevents you having everything you want in sufficient abundance and profusion to cause you to want to be reading this book (still)?

Absolutely nothing. However ...

happiness is a stupid thing to try and manifest as it comes and goes of its own accord, and trying to become attached to it when it comes only leads to disappointment when it goes.

you probably enjoy wanting more than getting

It's true; as daft as it seems, you might actually prefer the set of endorphins – the internal drug cocktail – that is released when you want something, to the set released when you actually get it. Which, in fact, is totally understandable. For a start, it's a state you're familiar with, and however much you may hate it, deep down you love it really – simply because our innate nature is to cling to and love what is, no matter how turgid it may be – that's the glue nature uses to organize itself into form and shape. Secondly, you know that as soon as you get what you want, not only will you have to deal with a new batch of responsibilities, but you'll have to deal with the disorientation of the new and the grief of letting go of the old, because you fear change and ultimately death (which all change finally leads to).

So you invent – at the deepest level of being, with all the backup of proof from years past, all the way back to the womb – reasons you can't get what you want, reasons which normally fit into two categories: I don't deserve it and I'm not capable of it. These categories then subdivide into more insidious beliefs, including: it's not fair to others who have less if I have more – I'll be depriving them of theirs; this world is hostile and unforgiving and won't give me what I want; others will be envious and hate (even destroy) me if I get what I

our innate nature is to cling
to and love what is, no
matter how turgid it may
be.

want; and even if I get what I want I'll still be miserable.

And while you may be tempted to examine your own reasons in depth, in faux-psychotherapeutic fashion, I wouldn't advise it right now, as what we're concerned with here is not how you got into gaol, but how to get out. The door is open, and the first step is to look around you (literally and metaphorically) and accept (fully, with all your heart, soul and might) that ...

you've got exactly what you want here and now

If you buy the original premise that you create your own reality, that your external conditions are a direct result of the beliefs in your mind, then it's fairly obvious that what you've got here and now is precisely what you want, even if it sucks. If you don't accept that, then you don't believe you create your own reality and if you don't believe that then you won't be able to use *wu wei* to get what you want from here on in, because you'll not be in a position of power. So you have to accept that what you've got is what you want in order for it to be changed or improved from this point on, according to your changing wants.

So there you are, that's it, you've already got exactly what you want. Sorted. So stop reading, put the book down and go and enjoy yourself. However, before you do, there are just one or two little things I should tell you.

Well, quite a lot actually, starting with the idea of having an ...

empty mind

According to the precepts of the *wu wei* way, once you've relaxed yourself enough to dance with the Dinner Lady, you then have to empty your mind. So go on, empty your mind now. Done? No, of course not, because emptying the mind is one of the trickiest things a person can attempt on this planet. However, don't be deterred by that. Indeed, take it up as a challenge and go to it with gusto, because until you manage to achieve an occasional fleeting moment of silence in there, your *wu* simply won't *wei*. This is because to manifest what you want you first have to have a clear picture of what it is, and you can't have that if your mind is full of interference. That would be like listening to the cacophonous sound of two tunes playing at the same volume at the same time. I say to manifest what you want you have to first have a clear picture of what it is and you can't have that if your mind is full of interfer-ence.

emptying the mind is tricky, but it's not impossible and is, once you get the knack, actually extremely simple.

To start with you have to believe that you can control your own mind, rather than the other way round. Now there are a thousand and eight different techniques from a plethora of spiritual disciplines to help you do this, including, for example, the following.

Imagine yourself standing by a river and throwing each thought, as it arises, into the current to be swept away.

Simply watch each thought arise from the nothingness and disperse again, making sure you catch the dispersal in case you lose yourself in the thought and get carried away.

Count your in and out breaths from one to nine and start again, or one to one thousand and eighty if you like, starting again at the beginning every time you get lost in a thought, visualize an extremely deep, dark hole, repeat, silently or aloud a mantra (sacred sound), such as:

Om (approximately, the sound of the Universal Dinner Lady's belly rumbling) imagine yourself standing by a river and throwing each thought, as it arises, into the current to be swept away.

Om mane padme hum (approximately, I surrender to the thunderbolt in the void)

Om shanti (approximately, peace)

Nam yoho renge kyo (approximately, I surrender to the law of cause and effect)

Gaté, gaté, paragaté, parasamgaté, bodhisvaha (approximately, go, go, go beyond, go beyond the beyond – to you (inside) who goes, I bow down)

Fortuna, Fortuna, give me my sweetcorn and tuna (approximately, goddess of good fortune, give me sustenance), or whatever you like really, as long as when you repeat it over and over, it cancels out the thoughts in your forebrain.

Or you can simply say to your mind with utmost authority, compassion and firmness, 'Shut the f*** up!' (which is approximately how I do it).

Whichever way you choose, and it really doesn't matter which, as long as you achieve even brief moments of emptiness, start practising immediately and continue till you die, if you really want to ...

form a clear picture now in order to get what you want

Come on, let's do it. But let's do it methodically, using the (carefully considered) aforementioned template. Let's conjure up a complete internal experience of what you want to manifest now, in full Technicolor, sensaround, 7.1 Dolby surroundsound, complete with smell, feel and taste, starting with:

clean air

Picture yourself always breathing clean air now – feel it thrill your lungs and oxygenate your brain – and picture it following you wherever you go. We have to start here with the basics and nothing is quite as basic, not only to your surviving but to your thriving, than breathing clean (or relatively clean) air, at least while you're on the planet. Moreover, by visualizing yourself breathing clean air, it's more likely you'll manifest realtime locations at which you'll be able so to breathe.

pure water

Picture yourself always drinking and having easy, uninhibited access to pure, or relatively pure, drinking water now – feel it caress your oesophagus as it slides down. While this may have not yet been something you actively craved, there is every likelihood, without wishing to alarm you, that before very long, relatively pure water for drinking and cooking will become more and more scarce on the planet, so visualize well, my friend, and you may even manifest a pure water spring in your own backyard.

uncontaminated food

Picture yourself always eating the finest (uncontaminated) food, your table laid with a feast fit for a queen or king. See the vividness of the greens, the depth of the browns, golds and yellows, the lushness of the reds and oranges; imagine the smell of it wafting sensuously up your nostrils, the taste of it bringing pleasure to your palate and tickling your tongue. Visualize well, for as with water, clean, wholesome food will become harder and harder to come by as time goes on and a steady supply will be extremely beneficial to your ongoing wellbeing.

shelter

While it's true that the essential purpose of shelter is to give you adequate protection from the elements as well as privacy, your home (or homes) also affords you the space to play out the theatre of your being, complete with props, sound effects and lighting. So don't hold back as you visualize this, your perfect home or homes, located, aspected, designed, furnished, equipped and externally landscaped exactly as you'd like. Go into as much detail as you can muster, all the way down to the finish on the plug sockets, the feel of the bed linen, the width of the TV screen, the colour of the walls and floors, the shape of the swimming pool, the heat of the steam room and the green of the foliage as the breeze blows through it. See yourself with key in hand, opening the door and stepping in – smell it, run your fingertips along the worktop surfaces in the kitchen, gaze at your reflection in the bathroom mirror and tiptoe proudly through the tulips in the yard.

clothing

(including, for the sake of convenience, shoes, accessories and all hair, skin and bath products, perfumes, tweezers, nail clippers, razors and all the gubbins you need to make you feel presentable)

While the essential purpose of clothing is to protect you, both from the elements and from being arrested (other than in your own home or equivalent, or designated nudist areas), we wouldn't have such a huge global fashion industry had we not the compulsive proclivity for dressing up for the purposes of impressing each other; and while it's possible you're so enlightened you don't do that too, it's unlikely, so visualize your wardrobe now, full of the most beautiful clothes and footwear you can possibly imagine and your bathroom shelves stocked with all the products you could ever want to pamper your beautiful body. See yourself stepping out in all your manicured finery (or neo-hippie throwaway chic, or however you fancy yourself looking), feel the fabric against your moisturized skin, the leather around your pedicured feet.

visualize your wardrobe now, full of the most beautiful clothes and footwear you can possibly imagine.

physical warmth

See log fires, underfloor heating, double glazing and roof insulation for the winter and warm sun on your shoulder for the summer, or however you like to take your physical warmth. See yourself now never having to shiver in discomfort – except, of course, on the rare occasion the boiler breaks down and you get ripped off by the plumber, for which occasional, inevitable eventuality, even the power of *wu wei* is no match.

physical comfort

While you'd think this would be covered by a combination of the above, comfort within your skin also depends on how flexible, supple and hence pain-free your body is, so visualize yourself being as loose as a long-legged goose without an ache or pain anywhere on your person – not just in an abstract way – actually visualize each limb and sector relaxed, supple, flexible and pain-free, and don't just visualize it but feel it from within as well.

strength

No need to explain why you need to include strength in your list of things to manifest. If you're not strong, you're weak, and if you're weak you won't stand up to the force of the world, which grows stronger the more you manifest, and life will simply knock you over. Strength here applies equally to mental strength and physical, though generally, mental strength comes from if you're not strong, you're weak, and if you're weak you won't stand up to the force of the world.

physical strength (and to some extent vice versa). So visualize those back muscles strong as an ox, those rippling biceps and quadriceps, those flabless abdominal muscles and proud pectorals, and don't just visualize them but feel them from within, rolling the concept out to include every sinew, nerve, bone, organ, blood vessel, sense organ, skin surface and all other constituent parts of your body. Be strong, comrade, sister or brother – the revolution needs you.

stamina

Wu wei or not, you'll need stamina to do everything you'll need to to manifest what you want – even to get through the day in a straight line you need stamina, so visualize yourself now tireless, indefatigable and with boundless stamina – enough to move ten mountains, not just one. And don't just visualize it but feel it collecting and storing itself in your bones and tissues, especially your thighs, which provide the perfect repository.

energy

Well, obviously you have to have access to limitless energy or you'd flake out before anything good happens; as well as which, you need energy to support your visualization, specifically in connection with utilizing the micro-cosmic loop for manifesting purposes, a process to be explained shortly. So visualize yourself imbued now with infinite energy –

visualize yourself imbued
now with infinite energy.

see it filling, supporting and surrounding you, perhaps as light, perhaps as an invisible vapour – that's up to you – and don't just see it but feel it too, for as you see and feel, so will it be (you create your own reality), and see yourself thus imbued, supported and surrounded until your dying day as there's no point programming yourself to flag when you get old or you won't be able to enjoy whatever it is you're manifesting.

health

Without preamble, visualize a rich golden fluid – the golden elixir of life – entering through the crown of your head, pouring down through your brain into your neck and through your throat into your body; through your heart, lungs, liver, spleen, kidneys, bowels, sex organs and all the other bits and pieces; through your arms, hands, hips, thighs, lower legs and feet; bathing every cell as it goes, renewing each one and making you well. See yourself enjoying robust health as you wander about your perfect home, energized, strong, full of stamina, wearing fine kit and smelling sweet.

longevity

While you may find it presumptuous to consider the possibility of extending your lifespan by choice, and while you may well be right, you might as well throw it into the mix anyway as there's nothing to lose in doing so and possibly many years of extra life to gain. I do it all the time and am still going strong at 153 – and

see yourself enjoying
robust health as you wan-
der about your perfect
home, energized, strong,
full of stamina, wearing fine
kit, and smelling sweet.

and feeling damn chipper too, I might add. So without further ado, visualize your cells reprogramming themselves for an extra lifespan now. See, if you'd care to be so bold, yourself dying hale, hearty and ready at the ripest of old ages with a broad smile of utter fulfilment on your face – why not?

physical beauty

While you may think there's something beautiful about being ugly, there obviously isn't or we wouldn't call it ugly. But before going any further, I must insist here that physical beauty, while obviously enhanced by such conventional considerations as symmetry of feature and buffness of muscle, is not solely dependent on them. On the contrary, physical beauty – the effect that makes people love to rest their eyes on you – comes from projecting your innate spiritual beauty through your features and body. So even if you've not been blessed (or possibly cursed) with perfect form, you can still enjoy projecting beauty exactly as you are to increase your lovability levels, which after all is why people want to be beautiful – so they can be more lovable and hence more loved. To which end, visualize yourself now radiating so much beauty as you wander in health about your perfect home and abroad, that all who lay eyes upon you feel instantly blessed, as if having just seen an angel from heaven. And don't just visualize it, feel it spread across your face and body as a discernible glow now.

confidence

Without confidence, the Dinner Lady will pass you over in the queue. Confidence is perhaps the main part of your side of the bargain. It means literally holding the faith with or in yourself, and if you don't have faith in yourself, no one else will either, and opportunities, which after all come to you through the agency of other people, will pass you by. If, on the other hand, you maintain the faith with yourself more or less consistently, others will too, and opportunities will befall you at every step along the Great Thoroughfare. So, without hesitation now, visualize yourself imbued with supreme confidence, see how it sits on your features and how it animates your body language – not with arrogance, but with dignified humility. See how it shines through your eyes – hear how it gives timbre to your voice.

freedom of movement
(including viable transportation methods)

While you may take freedom of movement for granted, the wisdom of historical perspective says you shouldn't. Freedom is a relatively new experience for humans who tend to default to restricting themselves and others at every bend in the road. So visualize yourself now with immunity from all restrictions to your free passage wherever you may wish to travel – no road block, border, traffic jam, river, mountain or ocean can impede your progress, as if you have the power to make yourself invisible and thus slide easily past any if you don't have faith in yourself, no one else will either.

obstruction – and don't just see it, but feel the thrill of it in your body now too.

sex

Almost everyone, including Mother Nature herself, agrees sex is, or at least can be, one of the most exciting, nurturing, life-affirming and of course life-generating activities on offer, but because it ideally involves the willing cooperation of another person (or persons, if you're greedy that way), it naturally tends to be a tricky thing to negotiate at times. So gird your loins and without indulging in sentimentality or mastur-batory fantasy (for now) visualize yourself enjoying a magnificent, multiorgasmic, healthy (disease-free and hangup-free) sex life without shame, guilt or fear. And don't just see it – smell it, taste it, hear it and feel it – feel it move through you like a vapour of personal sex-iness right now, you sexy beast.

empathetic company
(human warmth)

Without this, unless you've achieved ultimate mastery of self and are able to meditate for months on end in the unquestionable rarified bliss of solitude, which is pretty unlikely, you soon wither, go insane and die. So see yourself now, surrounded and supported by a net-work of compassionate people, including lovers, part-ners, family, friends and associates, with whom you have total empathy, and feel the warmth it generates visualize yourself enjoying a magnificent, multiorgasmic, healthy (disease-free and hangup-free) sex life without shame, guilt or fear.

in your heart and soul. See yourself wandering along
the Great Thoroughfare of Life attracting empathetic,
kind and loving company wherever you go.

freedom of ideas

No one enjoys having their thoughts restricted by having a limited model of reality. No one wants their imagination to be fettered by negativity. Everyone wants to
be creative, in their thoughts at least. Freedom to use
your imagination fully to conceive any old idea you like
is a great treasure and one you can access immediately now by visualizing yourself as being like Einstein,
with full freedom of imagination and full access to all
the creativity in the universe. Imagine the top of your
head wide open and downloading data even as we
speak.

freedom of choice

This is a big one. If you lived in a police state, your
freedom of choice would be far more limited, far more
underground than it is now. But even in liberal soci-
eties, we have a habit of restricting our own range of
choices by refusing to use our imaginations properly.
This in turn limits the range of experience at our disposal, which is a major cause of the endemic scourge
of depression afflicting our society these days – ironic
at a time when it would appear the range of experi-
ences on offer has never been so great. Visualize
yourself now as someone who knows they have

visualize yourself as being like einstein, with full free-dom of imagination and full access to all the creativity in the universe.

absolute freedom of choice – see how it sits on your features, how it animates your body and gives timbre to your voice. See yourself with the whole world at your feet here and now.

freedom of expression

Everyone loves a good natter. Everyone loves to get their view across. Again, this is something we take for granted but which is, in fact, a rare treasure. Opposition not only comes potentially from without, but also from within through lack of confidence or communication skills. So see yourself here and now with absolute freedom of expression, conveying your message through all appropriate means (verbally, musically, visually and so forth), with ease, clarity and grace, and see yourself being willingly received and understood.

love

If you were feeling sentimental or in a particularly retro-Beatles frame of mind, you'd stick this at the top of the list even before pure air, because without a doubt, the need to both give and receive love (to and from everyone) is the subtext of all our interactions with others – not that I'd say it's all you need, because without clean air, something to slake your thirst, a bit of grub in your stomach, a roof over your head, freedom from pain and illness, strength and all the rest of it, you won't be feeling very loving; and without some nice threads and a bit of a wash every now and then you won't be very appealing in the loveability stakes anyway. But once the basics are taken care of or transcended, it's love you want, not just carnal or romantic love but the unconditional, universal variety, as well as general day-to-day bonhomie. So visualize yourself now, chest completely relaxed, heart open, with love not only pouring forth from you, but pouring forth into you from six billion people worldwide including partners, lovers, family, friends, acquaintances and strangers, and don't just see it, but feel yourself veritably glowing with it now.

respect

Pretty much all the trouble and strife, the rage, the violence and the war comes about because someone feels someone else doesn't respect them in some way or other. Everyone wants respect – it's almost crucial to psychological survival – and to get it, as you know, you have to give it, not just to others, but most importantly to yourself. But what does it look like? I don't know – you'll have to make up your own picture – but do it now. Visualize yourself fully worthy of respect, respected and respectful, like an oriental master (or mistress) of some ancient, arcane art, with that air of respect hanging lightly but unquestionably around your person – and feel how it subtly alters your demeanour now.

visualize yourself now, chest completely relaxed, heart open, with love not only pouring forth from you, but pouring forth into you from six billion people worldwide.

everyone wants respect –
it's almost crucial to psychological survival – and to
get it you have to give it,
not just to others, but most
importantly to yourself.

gainful, fulfilling employment

Though you may well think it would be nice to lay around in bed all day (especially if you wake up tired in the morning), you'd probably find it a tad tedious after a few days, as anyone unfortunate enough to be bedridden will tell you. No, it's a fact, people like to be employed, and need to be – not just for obvious reasons of survival, for even those blessed or cursed with large inheritances crave a purpose in life, and purpose generally tends to be intimately tied up with gainful, fulfilling employment. Indeed, from my own perspective, I'd say it's one of the best drugs around, and seeing as you generally have to spend such a large slice of your available time doing it, it would be just as well to enjoy what you're doing. So visualize yourself now, doing exactly (or even approximately) the kind of work you imagine bringing you both the money you need and the fulfilment you crave, and if you already have that, visualize yourself refining it, so you earn even more and enjoy it even more profoundly. And don't just see it, but smell it, hear it and feel it too as a vapour of utter satisfaction pervading your person from head to toe.

social status

There's no need to point out how important social status is to everyone, even if they don't admit it. Our entire social structure, whether we like it or not, is organized around hierarchies of social importance, based on criteria of merit, wealth, power and influence (including the ability to provide connections through marriage or association). Were it not so, everyone would drive around in identical cars and wear identical clothes and have identical exteriors to their houses, and we wouldn't have such a sick fascination with celebrity culture, with all its shallow tawdriness. The energy we put into outward displays of status, however discreetly splurged, is truly phenomenal – hence the pointless expenditure on so-called premium logo branded clothing, for example, or being seen at the 'right' overpriced restaurants and clubs. And while it's obviously utterly silly, it's an utterly silly life in many respects, and nothing is gained by avoiding the status game altogether, so you might as well visualize yourself now enjoying good social standing and having the power to influence events in a positive direction. I'm not sure how that looks to you. But however it looks to you, let yourself see it, feel it, smell it, taste it and hear it now.

a good reputation

Having a reputation as a mostly (no one's perfect) honest, just and fair-minded person, as opposed to a dishonourable, no-good lying cheat, is not only desirable but fairly indispensable (unless you live in a bubble), for your very survival depends on people being willing to engage in commerce with you in one form or another and commerce depends on trust. So visualize yourself now enjoying a solid reputation as an all-round honourable character with whom others are keen to be involved on whatever level. Perhaps see yourself walking through the great marketplace of life and being greeted left, right and centre as a queen among women or a king among men – or even a queen among men and a king among women (or it could all turn out to be a bit of a dry experience for everyone).

popularity
(maybe involving fame)

Everyone except the most miserable spoilsport wants to be popular. Popularity is almost akin to respect, status and having a good reputation but is subtly different, in that when you walk into a crowded room, people don't just treat you with respect, admiration or at least deference, but come up and hug you instead, which is always a lot more fun for everyone involved. Indeed it's great to be popular, as long as you remember people are fickle and resist the temptation to take it seriously. So visualize yourself with a scintillating social life, the most popular belle or beau of the ball, your card marked for the duration, but visualize it so because you're exuding so much love and bonhomie. More importantly, visualize yourself with at least a few real friends, sisters and brothers who make your heart sing whenever you meet, talk, email or text, because as far as I can tell, all the clever-clever stuff aside, there's hardly anything more important.

safety

Interesting one, safety. Even though we know that living in a human body on a planet in deepest, darkest space, which is hurtling around the nearest star at 66,000 mph, while simultaneously rotating on its own axis at no less than 1000 mph, and is subject to the vagaries of stray asteroids and comets, unpredictable weather and climate, tidal waves, flooding, drought, famine, pestilence, economic turbulence, social unrest and human violence, is probably the most dangerous game a spirit can play in life, still we delude ourselves into expecting safety in our everyday lives and are strangely surprised when events turn dangerous. Nonetheless, start immediately visualizing a protective sheath of energy around you and anyone whose safety you may be concerned about. See yourself so surrounded, walking through the jungle of life without a single lion, tiger, mugger, rapist or murdering gangster pouncing on you now.

entertainment

Well it would be pretty damn boring without it, wouldn't it? No matter how spiritually developed you are, nor how fully engaged you are in your gainful, fulfilling employment, you still need to be entertained by life, whether formally at the theatre, movies, lapdancing club, comedy store or wherever, or informally by the living theatre, movie, lapdance and humour of everyday life. Essentially, most entertainment boils down to visualize yourself with at least a few real friends, sisters and brothers who make your heart sing whenever you meet, talk, email or text, because as far as I can tell, there's hardly anything more important.

watching other people do things that make you laugh, gasp or simply engage your attention so you can forget your own story for a while. See yourself being fully entertained and amused by the ordinary details of workaday life, as well as by troupes of the best performers of every showbiz discipline from every corner of the globe – why not? – and bring on those dancing girls (or, of course, boys).

a feeling of belonging
(wherever you are)

While it is evident on close inspection that even the most permanent object, such as the oldest mountain, was once nothing more permanent, hence belonging only in situ, than molten lava, we still delude ourselves into craving a sense of belonging on the planet, and specifically to a particular place or group of places and, even more specifically, with a particular person or grouping of persons. Of course when you see through the illusion, it's quite clear that if we belong anywhere at all, it's in our bodies and in the universe. Anything more defined than that is asking for trouble. Yet ask for trouble we always do – hence xenophobia, nationalism and all the painful nonsense that comes with them.

So visualize yourself now feeling a deep sense of belonging in your body in the universe, so that no matter where you find yourself, nor with whom, whether in

Taunton or Timbuktu, whether with friends or complete strangers, you feel completely at home. Feel it as a relaxing awareness in the belly now.

peace of mind
(including being at peace with the idea of dying one day, as well as having a workable, reliable philosophy or existential model that may or may not have spiritual underpinnings)

This is really the big one, because if you have unshakable peace of mind, no matter your external condition or situation, no matter your state of health, wealth or status, then you'll always feel comfortable, which is after all what everyone wants to feel all the time – comfortable. Peace of mind isn't something come by easily yet it is incredibly simple to attain. And it usually only takes thirty years or so of diligently following any valid psychophysical, spiritually based, philosophically sound system that grabs your fancy. Meantime, start visualizing yourself immediately with a mind so calm and peaceful that even if a stray asteroid were to crash into the ground before you now and destroy everyone and everything you hold dear or are familiar with, you would still retain your inner and outer composure – imagine *that*.

purity of heart
(hence authenticity and intensity of experience)

It's a rare person who'd enjoy an insipid life and who'd prefer things to be dull. Rarer still someone who'd truly

67

if you have unshakeable peace of mind, no matter your external condition or situation, no matter your state of health, wealth or status, then you'll always feel comfortable.

prefer simulated life to the real thing. Even the most commited couch potato, if you could get them up off their arse, would rather be out in the world having a good time than watching other people doing it on TV. But the intensity of experience we crave and look for mistakenly in drink, sex, drugs or spending money to excess, to name but a few examples, can only truly be accessed with a pure heart. This implies a sufficient level of inner self-awareness to be honest with yourself and hence honest with others wherever and whenever possible, something usually facilitated by a few years of therapy with a competent therapist, meditation under instruction from an experienced teacher, or both. Meanwhile, immediately start visualizing yourself with absolute self-honesty, purity of heart in other words, living each and every moment with optimum authenticity and hence intensity now (however that may look to you).

lots and lots of fun, laughter and smiles

To be honest, if you can successfuly visualize and bring into manifestation all the above, you shouldn't have too much trouble with this one. Nevertheless, it's useful to visualize yourself enjoying it all with ample fun and laughter just in case you forget. And if you forget to enjoy what you manifest, there's not that much point getting busy manifesting it in the first place – you might as well have stayed in bed after all and left the

Earth's resources that bit less disturbed. So see your-self now, laughing from the belly at the magnificent humour of it all and feeling the exhilaration of child-hood at simply being alive. See yourself enjoying it from this moment on – each and every second of it, no matter what, for as you see, so will it be, and you can't do better than that.

and of course, loads and loads of money

Yes, it's true. You may think money's a dirty business, but money is only a symbolic measure to help people do trade with each other. If we didn't have money, we'd only have to invent a new form of exchange, as there are way too many of us to barter for everything we need efficiently, and in any case the tax man would knobble you if you tried. Money's not dirty – it's the greed, fear, envy, hatred and violence it provokes that's dirty, but don't let any of that spoil your fun. In fact, money is a symbol of energy, hence why it's called currency, because it flows through society just like energy does, and as energy is essentially divine, so is money. So money is a symbol of the divine and is well worth manifesting in your life, not that you prob-ably need much persuasion – everyone loves money. The key is to get it to love you too. So saying, visual-ize yourself now as an extraordinarily powerful human magnet (or even magnate if you fancy), but one which attracts currency instead of metal, and see it coming

start visualizing yourself
with absolute self-honesty,
purity of heart, living each
and every moment with
optimum authenticity.

to you at high velocity in high denomination notes, in whichever strong currency or currencies you fancy, until you have tens of millions of the stuff sticking to your person, and if you keep visualizing it, within only days you'll notice an upturn in your financial fortunes – but we'll get on to time frames later.

And because all this comes with an underlying drive to continually improve the quality of each aspect once you have it, and usually to increase the quantity as well – more, more, more, in other words – remember you can tweak, refine, improve or even radically alter the entire visualization as often as you like, whenever you like.

In fact, you should be prepared for a long phase of perhaps a few years before your visualization settles into a steadyish shape. Luckily the Universal Dinner Lady won't penalize you for that, however, so don't be afraid to be flexible; in fact on no account be rigid about it or you'll spoil all the fun.

time frame

This is a very tricky business, putting a time frame round the picture, for no matter how well-visualized you are, you can't control the rate of manifestation. Nonetheless, without setting up some kind of time feel the exhilaration of childhood at simply being alive. see yourself enjoying life from this moment on – each and every second of it, no matter what, for as you see, so will it be.

frame, however arbitrary, it makes it difficult to put all the above into a unified shape, and it's essential to do that if you want to manifest it.

Probably the best and most workable way is to set up a frame of 1008 days – and remember this is just a device to enable your mind to put the picture in some kind of context. So you see yourself, imbued with all desired qualities of being, living out your desired scenario, complete with all the houses, equipment, personnel, shoes, handbags, tweezers and what-have-you within 1008 days – 87 days short of three years, in fact.

As you do so, you'll probably notice that all constituent parts of the visualization merge into a single image, perhaps of you standing beaming as you survey the interior of your house or thrilling to the view from your window, pretty much as I would be now were I not thrilling to the view of the computer screen instead. Perhaps you'll even feel the thrill of it in your chest as you do.

Fact is, it's perfectly OK to let the picture be fluid, indeed it must be as fluid as possible to accommodate the mysterious ways of the Dinner Lady, who after all has a mind all of her own. The important thing is that you see it at all and feel it in your body.

if we didn't have money, we'd only have to invent a new form of exchange. money's not dirty – it's the greed, fear, envy, hatred and violence it provokes that's dirty.

Once you see it, the key is to seal it, to turn it into an entity, as it were, and breathe life into it.

sealing the visualization

The most efficient way to seal your picture is to literally visualize a circular picture frame around it – perhaps a nice gilt one with '1008' running as a repeated theme pattern round the edges, and then to impose a symbol of your own choosing right slap bang in the centre of the image.

It doesn't actually matter which symbol you use. It could be your initials, for instance. It could be an om sign, it could even be a cartoonized picture of your own face winking back at you. Myself, I use the Barefoot Doctor star symbol, because for one, it's invested with a fair bit of magic of its own, and two, it sits with perfect symmetry at the centre of any visualization and helps draw the 'eye' there and thus focus the imagination.

Feel free to use it likewise (for visualization purposes only, of course – all use on commercial packaging strictly prohibited under trademark law, which has cost me a hundred grand to cover the entire world, so far, with the exception of a few places like Burundi, so don't be cheeky with my star, now, you hear?!) It really does seem to possess some kind of talismanic power of its own – which is not surprising if you knew the story surrounding me being given it, but for that you'll have to read my official autobiography when it's written; if you're interested, of course.

Whichever symbol you use, however – and you can change symbols as often as you like, though after a while it tends to help to stay with one – place it now in the centre of the frame to focus your mind while I explain the next bit.

dragging the visualization into your centre

This involves a touch of metaphysical dexterity. Basically, it involves grabbing the image in your forebrain and dragging it slowly and carefully into your lower abdomen, specifically just below your navel and about 16 cm back from the surface of the belly towards the spine, where you let it sit for a while and solidify, as it were, as you gather yourself ready for a spot of internal revolution.

You might, at this point, if feeling vaguely sentimental in a spiritual sort of way, make some acknowledgement to our Dinner Lady to secure her mandate for the whole procedure. Feel her loving eye upon you and your picture as this tends to warm things up a bit and that's important, because without warmth the whole experience becomes a bit lifeless and dull, which ultimately won't produce the scintillating results you're probably after.

Having collected yourself thus, you're now ready for the main action, which consists of concentrating deeply and ...

throwing it into the loop

... now, where was I? Ah, yes. Concentrating deeply now, breathe in and pack the breath, as it were, around the visualization in your belly. Now breathe out and as you do, let the breath push the visualization down between your legs. Now breathe in and let the breath carry the visualization up your spine to the top of your head, whereupon you breathe out again, letting the breath push the visualization down behind your face, through your throat and down the midline of the front of your body to between your legs.

Breathe in again, pushing the visualization up to the crown of your head and then out, pushing it down the

whatever you love will
blossom and bloom in
time.

front and so on, and do this nine times. With each successive revolution, the visualization becomes progressively more refined and concentrated. At the end of the ninth round, instead of taking it all the way down to between your legs, let the visualization rest in the centre of your chest and breathe normally, allowing all the details of the image to subside, leaving just your chosen symbol, which you allow to remain emblazoned on your heart.

It's crucial to let the image disperse, as this sets it free and enables all its constituent parts to travel to the Dinner Lady so she can make it happen. If you hang on to it, she can't do that and you've wasted nine good revolutions. However, it's also crucial to retain the symbol in your heart, as a receipt, to be imbued with your love – for as you know, whatever you love will blossom and bloom in time, as will the substance of your visualization now encoded in the symbol.

repetition

For best results, repeat the entire process of forming the visualization based on the original template and sending it into the loop with some regularity. This can be daily, weekly or monthly. Sometimes it will feel more real than others. Sometimes certain aspects will be more emphasized than others, almost to the point of being unrecognizable. The main thing is to keep doing it, for the more you do it, the stronger you'll become on every level and the more powerful will be your manifestation. Though in actual fact, it really only takes one fully conscious revolution of the visualization to make it manifest.

single aspect visualization

The above describes the process of manifesting the big picture over the course of 1008 days or thereabouts, the long haul in other words, and is based on the metatemplate of everything you want; however, you will no doubt also want to manifest specific aspects or details on a day-to-day basis. For example, you may want a startling love affair, not with anyone in particular – and indeed it is metaphysically unwise to specify the identity of any personnel involved in your manifestations, as this will inevitably entrap you in ways to be explained later – but perhaps you just fancy a startling love affair in principle.

So you follow the above guidelines and begin visualizing yourself doing whatever you imagine you'd do in a startling love affair (without forming a precise picture of the other party, simply sticking with the list of basic

qualities you'd enjoy in someone – availablity, willing-
ness, beauty, health, wisdom, kindness, sexiness,
sexual adeptness, intelligence, good sense of humour,
likes walking, movies, and warm nights in watching
telly or whatever, for instance). Perhaps you see yourself walking along the banks of the Seine, curling up
on a fur rug in front of a log fire in the Swiss Alps, gazing from the veranda of some palazzio or other on
Lake Como, or simply ripping each other's safari out-
fits off in the jungles of Borneo; you can make up your
own clichéd images for yourself.

You then frame the visualization, place your symbol in
its centre, grab the whole thing and drag it from your
forebrain down into your belly below the navel.
Breathe in and let the breath pack and compress the
visualization. Breathe out and send it down between
your legs. Breathe in and send it up your spine and so
on – nine revolutions around the microcosmic loop,
ending up in your chest, where you give the details of
the picture to the Dinner Lady, with only the symbol
remaining in your heart. Then go and polish your
shoes, dust off your party frock, suit, rubberwear or
whatever you're into and go and scrub up and sort
your hairdo out, as you can never tell how long it will
take to manifest – it may even be instantaneous, so be
prepared (and that includes condoms in this instance
too, don't forget).

visualize yourself doing whatever you imagine you'd do in a startling love affair.

do something

Don't be under the illusion that visualizing what you want, no matter how powerfully, replaces doing things in real time to make it happen. While it's true that at least 99 per cent of the work in getting something to manifest takes place internally, the remaining 1 per cent action is a huge 1 per cent. It's like the tip of an iceberg, which though perhaps only representing 1 per cent of the iceberg's total mass, would still hurt like hell if it fell on your head. In other words, there'll be lots to do, so don't get stuck on the idea of sitting on your arse all day waiting for things to happen.

Indeed, once you instigate any visualization process, you'll almost immediately start to feel urges arise in your belly, little prompts to go and do this or that. It may be a phone call, text message or email. It may be taking yourself off into town. It may be to catch a plane to Albuquerque or even Addis Ababa for all I know (though for me, it's usually Barcelona) – these prompts are your own business, but the point is to be alert and sensitive enough to discern them as they arise and to be courageous enough to follow them with real live action, for it is these urges and prompts that lead you to the opportunities through which your wants will be brought into manifestation. Or as Joe, son of Barefoot, my pragmatic eldest fruit of loin, says, 'There's no point sitting around all day reading books there's no point sitting around all day reading books about how to manifest things – just go out and do some work!

about how to manifest things – just go out and do some work!'

Enough said? Don't, in other words, use this manifesto as an excuse to be a lazy bum and then blame me when nothing special happens, because it simply won't do, comrade, sister or brother, that won't do at all.

timing

So how long does it take to manifest what you want? Obviously, this can only be accurately answered in ret-rospect, when what you've been visualizing actually comes to pass. To attempt to make timing forecasts is a game for fools. But being quite a fool myself, I would say that, generally, manifesting personal qualitites like strength, improved health, beauty, courage, clarity, or whatever, tends to be fairly instantaneous because there's only your own internal resistance to counter, as opposed to the much thicker, vaster, external resist-ance from the physical world around you.

However, it's fair to say that the more events and peo-ple required (in the external world) to bring something into manifestation, the longer it takes. Hence building or buying your dream house or houses (all finished, furnished and equipped, complete with all requisite whatever deadlines you set for any visualization to work for you, always be prepared to extend the deadline, indefinitely if needs be, without any shame, sense of failure or internal loss of face.

wardrobe, hair, bath and skin products, fragrance, tweezers and what-have-you; along with whichever car or cars you choose to ferry you around and all the other props and personnel you'll need to fulfil the having-everything-you-want scenario), which will require a multitude of events and people to be made manifest, will no doubt take a fair old while, even if you have the cash to pay for it all here and now. How long, though, is naturally impossible to say. If it's any guideline, my own visualization has taken no less than 20 years to manifest from scratch, and of course there's a lot of picture still to form and will be until I die (hopefully). But then, I'm a late developer and have often squandered energy on trivial pursuits, as well as which my visualization is so huge it's almost ridiculous and there's no reason your own visualization should take so long. On the other hand, it may take way longer.

Indeed, please remind yourself often that the aforementioned 1008-day manifestation period is purely arbitrary and only there to help lend shape to the picture. So whatever deadlines you set for any visualization to work for you, always be prepared to extend the deadline, indefinitely if needs be, without any shame, sense of failure or internal loss of face.

After all it doesn't really matter, for as I said, it's all only just a game you're playing to keep yourself entertained while you're hanging around waiting to die. So ease off worrying about timing now and relax into enjoying the process, something that will prove far easier for you once you fully appreciate ...

yin and yang and other vagaries of modern life

Without going into a full-blown, long-winded explanation of yin and yang and its vital importance in the Taoist scheme of things, whether following the *wu wei* way or simply doing nothing and gazing enlightenedly at your umbilicus, let it suffice to say that, whether looking through the eyes of Einstein or Lao Tsu (the big boys of modern western physics and ancient Taoist metaphysics respectively, hence they should know), all movement, all mass and all space – everything that happens in the universe no matter how massive or miniscule, that is – is governed by the eternal interplay of these two *a priori* forces or qualities.

By way of example ...

Yang represents the active, yin the passive.
Yang represents the dynamic, yin the static.
Yang represents a phenomenon's rising, yin its dispersal or dissolution.
Yang represents force, yin structure.

Yang represents the bright, yin the dark.
Yang represents the blatant, yin the obscured.
Yang represents the creative, yin the receptive.
Yang represents the full, yin the empty.
Yang represents the day, yin the night.
Yang represents the mountain, yin the valley.
Yang represents the hot, yin the cold.
Yang represents the new, yin the old.
Yang represents the hard, yin the soft.
Yang represents the transparent, yin the opaque.
Yang represents the wave crashing onto the beach, washing up your treasure, yin the wave ebbing and carrying all the pebbles, seaweed, broken glass, odd flipflops, jellyfish and other bits and pieces of beachlife detritus away.

Yin and yang are relative to each other. Take night, for instance, which relative to day is yin. You have bright yang spots at the city centre and dark yin spots out in the countryside. Or take a mountain (but watch your back) – the mountain is yang relative to the yin of the valley, but there's a dark side to every mountain where the sun doesn't shine, which is yin relative to the bright side that catches the sun all day.

You can't have one without the other. You can't, in the above instance, have a one-sided mountain and you can't have a purely dark night – well you could, but it would be well boring. You can't have day without

the Universal Dinner Lady
giveth and the universal
dinner lady taketh away.
having the good grace and
wisdom to accept that
will save you inordinate
amounts of unnecessary
grief, stress and anguish.

night, full without empty (otherwise where would you put it), force without form, new without old, and so on and so on. One turns into the other and vice versa.

More relevant to this manifesto, you can't just have wave upon wave crashing up on your shore without wave after wave ebbing away again, or you'll be flooded out of existence along with whatever treasure or pleasure has been washed up. The Universal Dinner Lady giveth and the Universal Dinner Lady taketh away. Having the good grace and wisdom to accept that will save you inordinate amounts of unnecessary grief, stress and anguish.

Moreover, the more our Dinner Lady takes away, the more she'll bring to replace it with (as long as you dance nicely, that is). Conversely, the more she brings, the more she takes away. Don't get stuck on either. Simply observe the phase of ebb and flow with compassionately detached serenity and humour. That's exactly why it's important to have a strong visualization to lend your will direction, so that no matter what comes or what goes with the crashing waves of the sea of life, you still end up manifesting, through thick and thin, precisely the life you want.

However, the motion of ebb and flow will give the appearance of slowing down the process of manifestation at times, which is why, for the sake of your sanity and equilibrium, you must accept its motion with equanimity and equipoise. Equally, be aware in an unequivocal and even equine, galloping, clippity-clop, nothing-gets-in-your-way sort of way, that come what may, yin phase or yang, you will get what you want, indeed have already got what you want, and the only thing stopping you enjoying it fully and improving it even more here and now is your own ...

resistance

To the extent you delude yourself at any one time that there's only the emptiness of yin and no fullness of yang, you descend into self-pity in any one of its insidious disguises, including indulging in feeling incapable of manifesting anything worthwhile; feeling unworthy or undeserving of it; feeling it would be unfair to others for you to get what you want if they're not getting theirs, hence afraid they'll envy, hate and ultimately destroy you; or feeling scared of change or allowing yourself to be overcome by sloth and apathy, all or any of which you then unconsciously project onto the world, and hence our Dinner Lady, who is always happy to oblige your fantasy and sets up obstacles in your path. Remember, you create your own reality.

remember, you create your
own reality.

However, practical consideration must also be given to the fact that things do actually take time to manifest, because of the physical, semi-solid nature of earthplane reality – you can't build a house in a second, in other words, but having spent many months building it, there will be one second in time, when the house is built and in that second, you can say its building is instantaneous. But to deny all the preparation that lead up to that point would simply be cheap showmanship. Likewise, you could say that all the invisible visualizing and hard work put in over the years to manifest your vision finally, instantaneously, springs forth as visible reality at a particular given moment in time, or you could say that was all just so many wasted words.

Either way, don't freak out about the fact of your resistance. Simply notice it, relax and carry on. This helps dissolve it gently, rather than trying to force it away. In actual fact, it doesn't matter how long it takes for your vision to manifest, does it? As long as you're occupied, engaged, amused and filled with a sense of purpose, you're getting value from it however little or much of it you've so far brought into material existence. Remember also, the result doesn't give you anything much more than results; it's all about enjoying dancing with the Dinner Lady.

don't freak out about the
fact of your resistance.
simply notice it, relax and
carry on. this helps dissolve
it gently, rather than trying
to force it away.

patience

Patience? What do you need patience for? Are you waiting for something to happen? If so, stop it immediately – waiting is an utter waste of time. It implies that something in your mind is more important than being where you are now, which is plainly silly as being where you are, here and now, there and then, is the only valid reality there is – everything else is mere fantasy until it comes to pass. Would you rather be somewhere else than where you are right now? If so, wish to be exactly where you are and accept full responsibility for having created it, no matter what an apparently lousy job you think you may have done, no matter how painful it may be to be there, because as soon as you accept that, you've put yourself back in a position of command, from which you're then free to re-create things along more agreeable lines. But don't sit there waiting for something – sure, be aware you want things and are expecting things to come about, but meanwhile get on with being here, because right now that's all you've got – which fact you'd realize soon enough if some bastard held a gun to your head and cocked the trigger. So be here now and enjoy it. And yes, I know I say all this is a game you're playing while hanging around waiting to die, but this is a highly poetic kind of waiting, while the other kind is simply prosaic and dull.

wish to be exactly where
you are now and accept
full responsibility for having
created it.

You don't need patience, you just need to breathe and relax.

maintaining the force of your visualization steadily and consistently

Because of the obstructions you create within and without, because of the fact of a whole series of moments in linear time being needed to build your house, so to speak, and because of the ebb and flow of yin and yang, during which your equipoise will no doubt occasionally be sorely challenged, unless you're already completely enlightened (in which case, why waste time reading books?), you will be required to access dedication, consistency in the face of an inconsistent world, courage, faith in yourself and humility in the face of the Dinner Lady, as well as any other qualities you can think of for yourself. In short, you must develop the power of unwavering intention.

unwavering intention

The Taoists call this 'i', pronounced 'eee', and consider it a force more powerful than daisycutters. While there's no short cut to developing some for yourself –

indeed many Taoists have devoted their entire lives to mastering the Taoist martial art Hsing I, spending many hours a day boxing shadows and other people, for the sole purpose of honing their 'i' (the 'i' of hsing i means 'intention boxing') – you can, however, make a grand start immediately by holding the symbol of your choice in the centre of your chest, while simultaneously holding a clone of it in the centre of your brain, and another in the belly below the navel, or simply let the one symbol in your chest stretch to include the centre brain and belly locations as well, and then proceed to hold it placed so pretty much all the time, for the rest of your life, no matter what else you may be engaged in or absorbed by at the time. Not only will this lend the necessary force to your vision but it will also imbue you with formidable focus and concentration in general – always a useful tool in such an unfocused and diffused world as the world of people.

But don't get too obsessed about it or you'll turn into one of those New Age weirdies no one wants to talk to, so filled with zeal for their sense of mission are they. Always relax and be soft about it. To help you do this, to reinforce your strength as you wander in the wilderness while our Dinner Lady prepares your feast, you can receive much sustenance along the way by learning to ...

always relax and be soft
about your intention.

read the signs

As soon as you instigate a visualization in the afore-mentioned manner, strange little synchronicities will start to occur; psychic slaps on the back to let you know you're on the right path. For instance, you may come out of your house just at the moment a truck goes by with the slogan 'You can have it all!' emblazoned on its side. Or you may adopt a set of confirmatory signs of your own. For me, every time I see a Parcelforce van (the UK version of a UPS or FedEx delivery van), I take it as a sign I'm about to receive an interesting invitation or offer. I then refine the sign by reading the numberplate quickly and whatever word springs to mind is then taken as a clue as to what kind of invite or offer it will be. Then they come in their white coats and take me away. But if you don't let yourself get too carried away, reading the signs can be most restorative on a low-faith, bad-hair kind of day; so read away, comrade, sister or brother, read away.

However, there's a far more powerful tool at your disposal, not only to maintain and strengthen your intention to manifest, but to pretty much take care of absolutely everything in your life with utmost efficiency and effectiveness and, though the very word may conjure for you awful images of silly alternative tossers kidding themselves about the reality of life, I must declare openly here and now that there's naught so powerful as doing ...

affirmations

I love affirmations and because I love them, they work for me. That's an affirmation, by the way. There's nothing new or particularly Californian about affirmations. Taoists have been using them in one form or another for millennia. So have all the Western spiritual traditions for that matter. Myself, I've been using them for nearly four decades, which is, I'm sure, part of the reason I've managed to live to such a ripe old age so far (153), and be in such good health and high spirits. While it's true that the mind is a terrible thing, once it's brought under your command, you can achieve anything you want (within the laws of physical possibility), hence the immense power of visualization.

But for most of us, holding the mind on a steady course through visualization alone is no mean feat. To help it along, as well as engaging in some sort of serious Taoist martial arts training – something I strongly recommend, no matter what your present physical condition or age, unless of course you're unfortunate enough to be bed-ridden or otherwise incapacitated;

something I never miss an opportunity to recommend, in fact, even when, as now, it bears almost no direct relevance to the subject matter – to help the mind along, the best thing you can possibly do is to engage in some sort of auto-suggestive technique. The most powerful of which, in my opinion, is the regular repetition of a series of affirmations, either written, spoken or even sung, and reinforced ritually by linking their repetition to various mundane activities, such as getting dressed in the morning or undressed at night, thereby providing triggers for your unconscious mind to make positive moment-to-moment choices.

They say it generally works best to repeat an affirmation a minimum of six times for it to truly penetrate the unconscious, but if you can just write down, speak or sing an affirmation once while fully visualizing what you're spelling out in words, that'll be sufficient to implant the command. For after all, that's what you're doing – commanding your mind to see something you want made manifest. And they're called affirmations because they imply saying 'Yes!' to life and the various aspects you're attending to. In fact, your unconscious mind only registers the positive part of any command. It ignores 'no', 'not', 'don't', 'won't' and so forth altogether. So if I say, 'Don't think about blue oranges!' you immediately think of blue oranges.

they say it generally works best to repeat an affirma- tion a minimum of six times for it to truly penetrate the unconscious. they're called affirmations because they imply saying 'yes!' to life.

Strangely enough, by the way, scientists have actually proven that oranges are in fact blue, for what it's worth – yet another example that all is not as it seems around here.

Hence it's essential that you phrase every affirmation positively. So, for example, if you want to give up drinking don't say, 'I don't drink now,' as this will merely translate as, 'Drink now!' Instead, say, 'I now enjoy drinking non-alcoholic drinks exclusively and my liver is much relieved!'

Notice how the affirmation is set in the present tense rather than the future. This is to encourage a visceral sensation of already having what you want, which in turn institutes an energetic, vibrational resonance that acts like a magnet, drawing the manifestation into your material orbit. It's also because the future doesn't exist and never will. The future can never be more than a concept in your mind. When the future arrives, it's already the present. The present is all there is, the past having gone already, hence the present is where the power to manifest is accessed.

So always construct affirmations in the present tense. Rather than saying, for example, 'I will achieve incredible amounts today easily and effortlessly,' say, 'I achieve incredible amounts today easily and effortlessly!' Rather than, 'I will live in a beautiful house one day,' say, 'I live in a beautiful house here and now!' Then, even if you live in a hovel, firstly, see the beauty in it and, secondly, superimpose the vision of a beautiful house over it and feel as if you already live in it. The more visceral you can make it, the more readily it will spring forth into manifestation. But don't give yourself a headache over it. Relax and do it gently, always.

If you're not feeling in the mood for metaphysics but simply want to focus your intention on manifesting what you want, say (in the above instance), 'I choose to live in a beautiful house now.' If you suspect you have issues about not feeling worthy to have what you want, say, 'I deserve to live in a beautiful house now.' If, deep down, you think living in a beautiful house will cause those who don't to suffer and feel deprived, say, 'By living in a beautiful house, I inspire others to make their own worlds beautiful and, because I feel more comfortable in mine, I become more creative, have more to offer and thus enrich my world and everyone in it.' At which point I must point out that you'd be best to compose your own affirmations in your own style to avoid falling into the trap of repeating such absurdly constructed sentences as the above.

always construct affirma-
tions in the present tense.
say, 'I achieve incredible
amounts today easily and
effortlessly!'

If you have an issue with your concept of the divine and believe it wants you to suffer, and that it's wrong to get what you want, say, 'My concept of God supports me getting what I want now.' This obviously applies to all internalized figures of authority, such as priests, teachers, parents, police, government and even the general public. Hence, in short, for example, 'The establishment wants me to get what I want now – society wants me to get what I want now – everyone wants me to get what I want now!'

'I am' is powerful too, as in, 'I am beautiful. I am magnificent. I am damn sexy!' (So are you if you want to be, by the way.)

Then there's putting the object of want first, as in, 'Money now comes to me in ever increasing amounts,' or 'Love now comes to me in satin sheets,' (though personally I've always preferred freshly laundered white Egyptian cotton).

Then there's the 'It's OK' style, as in, 'It's OK for me to be and feel magnificent in every way and live a magnificent life now,' or 'It's OK for me to feel sorry for myself as long as I find it enjoyable,' which is actually a damn good way of dealing with negative states when they come upon you. So, for example, 'It's OK for me to feel scared as long as I find it useful and enjoyable – likewise, angry, disorientated, miserable,

it's ok for me to feel sorry
for myself as long as I find
it enjoyable, is a damn
good way of dealing with
negative states when they
come upon you.

lonely, depressed, stressed or any other state I choose to explore.'

You know, I've never been one to dissect and methodically set out all the different styles of affirming things, even though I've tried many times, and while I openly admit this may well just be a cop-out, I instinctively feel it has more to do with not wishing to fully demystify the tradition of affirming, which, after all, has its roots all the way back in the very beginnings of time as we know and love it, with the Old Testament God, right at the start of Genesis, as in the genesis of existence, saying as his opening shot, 'Let there be light!' And while this isn't strictly an affirmation in the conventional sense, more a direct command to the light, which you must remember was, without getting theological on you here, within 'Him', it still fits into the general affirmation scheme enough for me to use it to justify the quasi-mystical quality of affirmations. Thus why I don't feel like laying the whole process too bare lest I destroy the magic for you. Which translates as my brain simply doesn't want to go there right now. Instead, and far more useful to you, allow me to present you with a slew of affirmations appertaining to the original 'wants list' template, along with explanations where appropriate, so you can start using them at once.

affirmation city

While it would be logical to follow the 'wants' template in an orderly manner here and offer up the appropriate affirmation to fit each stage of the visualization, I would grow bored very quickly like that, which I suspect means you would too. So if you'll indulge me here, I'd like to go into free flow and let the affirmations come as they will, just as if I were doing a personal affirmation session of my own, which to be really precise about it, at the time of writing – way before you'll be reading this, in other words – to all intents and purposes, is exactly what I am doing. That way it will be fresh and full of good chi, which will hopefully inspire and trigger the requisite sparkle in your own process of manifestation, should you be inclined at any stage – this one, for instance – to use any or all of them for yourself.

Just as a guideline, my own sessions, which I've done with varying regularity over the past three decades, and which I swear by as the most remarkable way of doing so-called magic, generally consist of half an hour or so spent with pen and paper, writing affirmations down as they occur. As well as this, I link certain affirmations with various chi gung standing poses as part of a daily morning routine to set me up with the right frame of mind for the day (or night). As far as this goes, it really makes no difference what action you my own sessions, which I swear by as the most remarkable way of doing so-called magic, generally consist of half an hour or so spent with pen and paper, writing affirmations down as they occur.

attach an affirmation the day (or night). As far as this goes, it really makes no difference what action you attach an affirmation to – it could be saying to yourself, for example, 'I have clear vision, I have strength, I know what I'm doing, and everything and everyone helps me succeed now,' as you take your first pee of the day. Personally, I do that one each morning with a hsing i shadow boxing posture beyond my powers of description to explain here but, as I say, which action you link your affirmation to is purely arbitrary.

The linking of a particular affirmation to a particular action on a daily basis serves well, in a cumulative way, to keep you in a manageable state of mind to deal with your life in general, whereas the concentrated affirmation writing sessions work along the lines of having a good heart to heart business meeting with our Universal Dinner Lady, during which you remain hyperconscious and with every expectation of achieving a miracle or quantum shift of circumstances.

At least, that's how it works for me. Feel free to invent your own way of dancing, although of course you are more than welcome to appropriate any or all of the following affirmations as your own. After all, they're only affirmations.

Talking of which, many people feel uneasy with affirmations because they think they encourage a form of denial about whatever's troubling you – and I won't deny that. For example, if you were feeling deeply depressed, they say it would be absurd and dishonest to affirm, 'I am feeling deeply happy,' and I totally agree. If, however, someone deeply depressed were to affirm, 'I choose to use this depression to grow stronger and more self-aware and by doing so I access my innate natural joy again,' they would be making the best of a bad job instead.

In other words, affirmations are not there to deny or obliterate negative belief patterns, but to transform them into something more useful to you. And talking of use, it surely must be time to experiment using a few affirmations yourself now.

So without further ado …

'I am alive.'

Go on, say it. I am alive. You think that's silly? Too obvious to make mention of? Don't be blasé, comrade, just say it a few times and see how alive it makes you feel.

'I go forth from this point fully trusting the Universal Dinner Lady to bring me everything I need, as and when I need it.'

affirmations are not there to deny or obliterate negative belief patterns, but to transform them into something more useful to you.

This is a good one to start the day with, as is the above. When you say it let your awareness expand to encompass the essential benevolence of existence, which you will feel like a blanket of love around your person. I won't keep saying, 'say it', but say it a few times now until it resonates with the truth inside you. And yes, this brings up the issue of need as opposed to want, which will be discussed later.

'With every breath I take, I am growing stronger, healthier, more vital, more vibrant, more energized, more inspired, more cheerful and altogether more magnificent at every level and in every way.'

That speaks for itself but, as you say it, visualize the breath as the catalyst that sparks up a moment of accessing those qualities, and any others you may care to add if you're in the market for making long lists.

'I always meet all my physical needs easily, effortlessly and enjoyably. I always water, feed, house and clothe myself (and any dependants) adequately, no matter what. I'm at home on the material plane – I love it and it loves me.'

It's important to make friends with material reality, so you stop mystifying and being afraid of it. This is tantamount to an agreement you make with yourself to steady your stance in relation to manifesting the basic requirements and, while basic, it is in no way something to be overlooked, so say it with enough gentle gusto and frequency for it to penetrate deeply into the hidden recesses of your psyche now.

'I am surrounded by people who love me deeply and care for my welfare – my world is a warm, nurturing place full of beautiful souls like me.'

Otherwise, your mind defaults to believing your world to be hostile, cold and uncaring, which then produces exactly that effect in the external world. So say it, even if right now you're suffering an 'I'm-all-alone-and-feel-ing-isolated-and-abandoned attack' and, as you do, allow yourself the awareness that there are six billion people on the planet with you right now, many of whom are willing and ready to reflect back at you whatever you project from your mind. So as you say it (write or sing it), project warmth, love and caring and, before you know it, you'll have it reflected back at you. Remember the whole affair is nothing but a vast hall of mirrors.

'The more I allow my human warmth and love to radiate naturally from me, the fuller my world becomes with warm, loving people.'

And see yourself surrounded now by an entire network of supportive, loving friends, all responding to the good energy you're emitting.

'I am totally at peace and nurtured on my own – I love myself so much it thrills me to be with myself – I am also delighted for others to come and share the fun whenever I feel like it.'

It helps, along with saying this, to relax your body and breathe enough to overcome any deep-seated fears you may have about being all alone in a big, bad world. As soon as you relax your body and breathe you see that any wobbly feeling arising in the belly and chest is only a wobbly feeling, which passes as you keep breathing.

'I am easy with any feeling that may arise within, no matter how strong or fearful – I just relax my body, keep breathing and trust all my needs are met. I've now overcome any compulsion to run away and hide from what I feel.'

Our whole culture is based on distracting ourselves and diverting awareness away from feelings. But as soon as you surrender to whatever you're feeling, rather than trying to fight it, the feeling evaporates and you return instantaneously to a state of wholeness and peace. You surrender by relaxing your body and breathing freely without holding your breath (except when under water or during chemical attack).

'All internal psycho-emotional discomfort evaporates now and I find myself at peace.'
'I determine what kind of life I have – no one and nothing else.'

Go on, comrade, you tell 'em! It's an interesting thing, this taking full responsibility for yourself. To stop projecting responsibility for yourself (and your moment-by-moment experience of life) onto other people – your boss, your lover, your partner, your mother, the government, the world in general – and say:

'I take full responsibility for myself and my moment-by-moment experience of life from this moment on.'

So if you wake up feeling happy, it's because you've managed to inject the right mix of internal chemicals into your bloodstream by having issued the right mix of thoughts from your brain to feel happy. Likewise if you wake up feeling fraught or frazzled. It has nothing to do with what's going on in your life externally and everything to do with how you respond to it – and maybe not even how you respond but how you proactively go out to meet it. So if you were to say:

'Today, I go out to meet life as a warrior and I choose to feel delighted by every twist and turn rather than feeling perturbed, because it's my choice and mine alone.'

Say it with enough gentle gusto to feel it as a truth and then keep reminding yourself of that choice through-out the day come what may ... if you were to say that, do you think you'd have a different kind of day than if you allowed your head to be ruled by the belief that you're at the mercy of external events and other people? I suggest you would have a much more fulfill-ing day that way on every level and, moreover, sug-gest you try it, or something similar instantly. This will be facilitated by your breathing deeply and slowly throughout, as this tends to calm your mind down, which is essential if you wish to fully flow with your tao right now.

'I achieve everything I need to to materialize my vision in this very moment, and every moment that follows, easily, effortlessly, enjoyably, swiftly and miraculously now.'

I must resist the temptation to try to sell you these affirmations, to attempt to enthusiastically convince you of how utterly efficacious they can be, as that tends to be rather crass all round – but this affirmation works so well, I can't hold back. If you can write, say or sing this one with enough presence of mind for it to penetrate, you will (probably) be utterly amazed at the results. Indeed, I'd say it was a major key to enlightened living all on its own.

'Even now, I am in the process of manifesting everything I want, including my perfect home or homes along with all the equipment (including dishwashers, hairdryers, irons, tweezers and so forth) and help I need to manifest everything else I want.'

or

'Even as I go about my daily doings, fulfilling all my mundane tasks and engaging in the details of my daily existence, the Universal Dinner Lady is making quantum events occur behind the scenes to bring my vision into manifestation now – what a blessed being be I.'

Yes, it's perfectly OK to have fun and talk in an arcane manner when 'doing' affirmations. You must always have fun, no matter what you're doing, in fact, or what's the point? So say:

'I now allow myself to have inordinate amounts of fun all the time now, no matter how seemingly turgid or painful my external reality appears.'

This 'allowing yourself' is a big thing too. You may not have realized it, till now, but the only reason you may not have enoyed yourself fully on the planet till now (assuming you haven't, of course) is that you haven't been allowing yourself to. You may have inherited this self-limiting way from your parents, teachers, siblings or peers and been hitherto unconscious of having done so, but that's no reason to continue to do so, so why not add:

'I now allow myself to live each and every moment at optimum levels from now on'

and

'I now allow myself to gain full entertainment and nourishment value from each and every moment as it happens, come what may'

or do you find that daunting? If so, say:

'It's perfectly fine for me to indulge in feeling daunted by the idea of enjoying myself all the time come what may, as long as I find indulging in feeling daunted enjoyable'

which will either clear things up right away or make you even more confused, in which case, say:

'I choose to access perfect clarity here and now'

or

'I am clear that the purpose of being on the planet is to enjoy myself from now on, come what may'

and if that sparks off fears that you'll run rampant and ride roughshod over others in the quest for enjoyment, affirm:

'By containing my energy and being kind, empathetic, responsive and compassionate towards others, I enjoy myself fully each and every moment I spend on this planet.'

Ah, yes, the planet. It's important to remind yourself where you are from time to time – it keeps you awake. It also reminds you of the choice you once made as a free-floating spirit in the ether, to take form at this time on this particular planet. You could have picked a zillion others, but you chose this one. Good call, comrade, sister or brother. Acknowledging yourself for that instantaneously increases your personal power levels, which in turn translates as energy, and it's that very energy the Universal Dinner Lady requires to take you seriously enough to manifest your vision for you.

Self-acknowledgement in general is a damn good thing, in fact. So much of the time we spend telling ourselves off, putting ourselves down and altogether making ourselves miserable as if it were some kind of duty or obligation, whereas it isn't. So is there any reason you can think of not to say the following (and mean it)?

'I acknowledge myself now for still being alive.'

What? Am I being serious? (I hear you ask). Yes, because though you may take still being alive for granted, it's actually a fairly tricky thing to achieve when you consider the huge array of forces lined up against you, ranging from asteroids to viruses, not to mention suicide bombers, gangsters, rapists, paedophiles, tax collectors, hurricanes, contaminated food, impure water, polluted air and all the other assorted dangers that have been threatening your survival each and every day since you were born (and not to mention your own self-destructive urges, too), and though you may think you had very little to do with surviving all that, think again, comrade, think again.

'I acknowledge myself for having the courage and endurance to carry on.'

Again, you may think it's something that comes of itself, this ability to carry on, but think back to the last time a mild or heavy free-floating depression wafted along your way and you just wanted to stay in bed and hide. Furthermore, realize that this fight to go on actually continues permanently on the deeper levels of consciousness, so give yourself the big-up for having what it takes to continue the game another day. In fact, reinforce that ability right now by affirming,

'I have the courage, endurance and strength to carry on, come what may.'

'I acknowledge myself for being able to communicate my needs and desires with sufficient clarity to have got this far.'

This leads us to the idea of other people and how you manage yourself around them, a crucial aspect of manifesting what you want, which will be discussed later in more depth. For now, consider how pretty much everything you want will come to you via the agency of other people, courtesy of the Universal Dinner Lady, whom, incidentally, I'm tempted to call UDL from here on in, but will resist for poetic reasons, feeling it makes her sound too much like a reactionary political party rather than the ineffable, ubiquitous, *a priori* force of unconditional benevolence that she is.

So how about, (and this works brilliantly):

'I now elicit happy and willing cooperation from others all the time, no matter what I'm doing, whom I'm with, or where I am'

or,

'I now allow others to cooperate happily and willingly with me.'

Notice how you're not thinking of forcing anyone to do something against their will, as that would only backfire on you in time. Instead, you always bear in mind that everyone has free will. You also train yourself to want only what's in accord with the way of the Universal Dinner Lady; so if you were to affirm something like:

'People now enjoy giving me bus-loads of money simply for being on the planet,'

an affirmation well worth experimenting with, you may be inclined afterwards to add:

'Everything I affirm is in accord with the free will of everyone and in accord with the way of our Universal Dinner Lady.'

or,

'I get what I want by the free will of everyone and for the highest good of all.'

Remember, you create your own reality, according to which set of beliefs you choose to subscribe to at any one time. You can alter the very foundations of your reality altogether and thus build a totally different and more useful belief structure that will produce magnificent results. In fact, don't just take it from me but affirm for yourself:

'I create my own reality according to which set of beliefs I choose to subscribe to now. I now alter the very foundations of my reality altogether and thus build myself a different and more useful belief structure that even now is producing magnificent results,'

and we all like magnificent results.

Or maybe you believe it's crass to enjoy results – perhaps you should enjoy suffering instead? Say:

'The more I enjoy the results of my affirmations, the more effectively they work for me.'

How good can you take it? Does the idea of having this much potential power over external reality scare you? If so, affirm:

'My affirmations only work when in accord with the Tao, Universal Dinner Lady, God, or any other model of the ineffable I may care to believe in.'

On the other hand, there's nothing wrong with feeling scared as long as you're enjoying it. Affirm:

'It's perfectly OK to feel afraid.'

Affirm that at least 81 times in a row and you'll feel yourself starting to relax about the whole idea of being afraid. Fear is only fear, after all. Why run away from it? Instead, enjoy the feeling of fear when it arises – at least it lets you know you're alive. Say:

'It's perfectly OK to feel afraid as long as I'm enjoying it.'

This 'as long as I'm enjoying it' device, when applied so that it allows you to carry on entertaining negative, unpleasant feelings, may at first confuse your mind. This is exactly what it's there for – to challenge the supremacy of the belief that you're somehow obliged to suffer. It can be applied to any negative or painful mind state you find yourself in. Hence:

'It's perfectly OK to feel angry as long as I'm enjoying it.'
'It's perfectly OK to feel stressed as long as I'm enjoying it.'
'It's perfectly OK to feel lonely as long as I'm enjoying it.'
'It's perfectly OK to feel depressed as long as I'm enjoying it.'
'It's perfectly OK to feel isolated as long as I'm enjoying it.'

'It's perfectly OK to feel irrelevant as long as I'm enjoying it.'
'It's perfectly OK to feel oppressed as long as I'm enjoying it.'
'It's perfectly OK to feel worthless as long as I'm enjoying it.'
'It's perfectly OK to feel stuck as long as I'm enjoying it.'

And so on.

On the other hand – and this tends to exert a quite powerful liberating influence on your person – try saying:

'It's perfectly OK for me to feel magnificent, beautiful, splendid and exhilarated all the time now.'

And don't just say it, but feel it with all your heart, soul and might, because it really is OK to feel that, no matter how much negative, self-limiting, self-torturing conditioning you may have brought with you over the years to the contrary.

But don't stop there, continue with:

'It's OK for me to feel sexy, confident and deserving all the time now,' and

'It's OK for me to feel damn chipper and fine now all the time.'

But then you may think, 'But what about all the poor people who are suffering at this very moment – how can it be OK for me to feel damn chipper and fine no matter what, with all that suffering going on? – maybe I should join them instead.' Which while perfectly understandable, laudable and compassionate, is misguided. You won't help the suffering people of the world by adding to that suffering with your own. In fact, you owe it to all your suffering sisters, brothers and potential comrades on the planet to feel damn chipper and fine all the time no matter what, as that increases the general joy levels which act as a magnetic pole that attracts more and more people to enjoying themselves. But then you may ask, 'But what about those who are in such dire conditions they can't do anything about it?' And it's true – there are people on the planet at the very moment you're reading this, hundreds of millions of them in fact, who are suffering unthinkable deprivations and pain, and it's a horrible truth indeed, but you really won't be helping their plight by making yourself suffer along with them. Yes, you feel compassion and empathy, hopefully more and more over time; and yes, you do everything in your power to relieve the suffering of others whenever the opportunity presents itself, but you do that far more effectively, in a state of cheerfulness and strength, than in a state of misery and weakness. When you feel miserable and weak, you don't feel like helping anyone, let alone yourself. So buck up and say:

'By allowing myself to feel damn chipper and fine no matter what, I am providing inspiration to others less fortunate than I at this time.'

Or,

'By allowing myself to feel damn chipper and fine come what may, I am raising general cheerfulness levels on the planet, which is ultimately better for everyone.'

Or even,

'I serve my all sisters and brothers best by being cheerful no matter what.'

Or simply,

'I am cheerful no matter what.'

But if you still find resistance to that idea springing forth from the bowels of your mind, simply as an experiment with reality, say,

'I allow myself to feel cheerful all the time now, no matter what.'

And,

'I deserve to feel cheerful all the time now, no matter what.'

And,

'I choose to feel cheerful all the time now, no matter what.'

And if that doesn't stir a slight sea change in your feeling tone, you might try the direct command approach instead and looking yourself straight in the eye, simply say, 'Oh cheer up, you miserable bastard, you!'

And if even that doesn't work, it means you have some relinquishing to do, along the lines of:

'I now relinquish all suffering.'
'I now relinquish all bogus beliefs that tell me I'm obliged to suffer here.'
'I now relinquish all self-limiting beliefs.'
'I now relinquish all self-punishing thoughts.'
'I now relinquish all beliefs that this is a hostile world.'
'I now relinquish all beliefs that tell me I can't get what I want.'

'I now relinquish all beliefs that tell me I shouldn't want to get what I want.'
'I now relinquish all beliefs that tell me I don't deserve to get what I want.'

And so on. But if you're really in the market for a bit of experimentation with reality, simply say:

'I now relinquish all beliefs!'

Because it's perfectly OK to simply be – to be without prejudgements, opinions and beliefs; to simply experience everything from a state of pure consciousness, or live in the pure land, as the 'Pure Land' Buddhists would say. Zen Budhists call it 'beginner's mind'. The Taoists simply say be like a child. And they don't mean a spoilt brat. Being like a child means being innocent and joyful like Pooh Bear, if you'll excuse me borrowing Benjamin Hoff's magnificent metaphor from *The Tao of Pooh*. Hence:

'I wander along the Great Thoroughfare of Life innocently and without preconceptions and marvel at the splendour of reality.'

Both Buddhists and Taoists would point out that this was a major key to enlightenment, and they'd be right on the money.

But you may believe that being innocent and like a child will leave you vulnerable to the evil intentions of nasty, twisted people along the way, in which case affirm:

'By allowing myself to be innocent and childlike as I wander along the Great Thoroughfare, I instantaneously develop a natural shield of energetic protection to keep me safe at all times, no matter what, where or when.'

Or simply,

'I am protected and safe at all times.'

Or even repeat over and over until it insinuates itself into your deeper circuitry:

'It's OK, It's OK.'

Because it is.

But talking about being right on the money, how about the whole issue of money in general, or more specifically personal wealth creation?

Well, how about starting with the following affirmation and seeing what it provokes or evokes?

'I love money.'

Do you find it sticks in your throat, after all those years of pretending to dislike it for fear of appearing somehow in bad taste or even evil? Go on, say it again and again a few times:

'I love money, I love money, I love money, I love money, I love money, I love money, I love money!'

Does it make you feel crude or in some way besmirched? (Don't you love that word!) If so, say (and this is perhaps my personal favourite money affirmation):

'I love money, money she loves me, we all love money and it's love that sets us free.'

It's actually a lyric from one of my tunes which I'd sing for you now if I could, and may well record for you one day, who knows even perform for you live but, until such time, perhaps you'd like to try singing it in a little ditty style for yourself. Come on – altogether now:

money is nothing more or less than a symbol of energy – energy we pass around the joint in the form of work done, time spent and attention paid – it is the symbol of the very currency or energy current flow of human society.

'I love money, money she loves me, we all love money and it's love that sets us free.'

That's good. And why is it good to love money? Because money is nothing more or less than a symbol of energy – energy we pass around the joint in the form of work done, time spent and attention paid. It is in fact the symbol of the very currency or energy current flow of human society. And that's a divine phenomenon – the sharing of energy between us all. So strip your concept of money of all negative connotations (love of money is the root of all evil and so forth), and start loving it now as a symbol of the divine instead – the fabric of the Universal Dinner Lady's apron, if you like.

And if you think that's the devil in me talking, you may want to consider a course of therapy at your earliest convenience. In fact, even if you don't believe in devils and other such nonsense, I'd still advise a course of therapy at some point in your life. No, not because you're crazy enough to be reading Barefoot Doctor books like this – not because you're crazy at all (I'm assuming), but because it's the most efficient way of having a panoramic view of your own internal reality models and hence provides you with a new sense of inner direction. But that's a whole other subject of its own – whether to spend some time in therapy or not – meantime, you can possibly save people love giving me loads of money simply for being alive.

yourself the thousands you'd end up shelling out for therapy by devoting half an hour, three or four times a week, for the rest of your life, to doing affirmations like these.

So saying, say:

'Money now comes to me in ever increasing amounts, with ever increasing velocity and speed, from every direction at once.'

And,

'My income now always far exceeds my expenditure.'

And,

'People love giving me loads of money simply for being alive'

(why not?) And,

'I now make loads of money doing what I most enjoy.'

Because it would be awful if you were still labouring under the delusion that you have to suffer by doing work you hate, just to make money. You should never do work or anything else you hate – it's a waste of time. If, however, you are currently positioned in a job you hate, stop hating it now by dislodging the hateful thoughts attached to it. Try,

'It's perfectly OK for me to waste my valuable time and energy hating the work I do, as long as I find that enjoyable.'

Or if that doesn't do it for you,

'I am now willing to enjoy whatever I'm doing, no matter what, because this is MY LIFE!!!'

And,

'By allowing myself to enjoy what's going on, what's going on changes of itself and becomes far more enjoyable.'

In other words, by surrendering to what's happening, desisting from fighting it, accepting and loving it as something you've chosen, what's happening stops feeling so hated, hence hateful, and starts acting more kindly towards you, as would anyone you started loving more. That's how the dance with the Dinner Lady works – love what is and what is transforms into something even better for you.

by constantly radiating
love, I am constantly
receiving it.

But don't just take that as empirical fact, experiment with it for yourself. Say:

'I now allow myself to love what is and what is now transforms itself into something even better.'

And while you may consider my repeated use of the word 'now' excessive, and while, stylistically, I totally agree, it is in fact a device to keep triggering the mind back into the present moment, which, as previously stated, is where the power to transform reality is to be found. So feel free to sprinkle it on your affirmations with gay abandon, now.

Now, we were on to the subject of love, which, after all, along with money is what everyone wants. Essentially they both boil down to the same thing – the passing of energy between people. But of course love also implies passing energy between us that is filled with warmth, kindness and life-affirming intention. That's why everyone wants it so much.

And as you know, the way you get it is to give it. So start off with something like,

'I am constantly radiating energy filled with warmth, kindness and life-affirming intention'

and then progress to,

'I am constantly radiating love.'

Then,

'By constantly radiating love, I am constantly receiving it'

and,

'I am loving, lovable and loved'

and even,

'I am love!'

Because you are – you are pure love in motion and if you don't believe me, say:

'I am pure love in motion,'

and,

'I am pure love in motion and wonderful things are happening as a result even as I say this affirmation.'

Talking of which, if the bowels of your mind are starting to throw up resistance to the whole idea of affirmations, in the guise of cynicism, say at this point,

'I create my own reality according to which set of beliefs I choose to subscribe to. By writing, saying or even singing affirmations, I am merely confirming that I'm choosing to subscribe to a set of beliefs that serve me better.'

So saying – and back to the relinquishing format here – say:

'I now relinquish all beliefs and concepts that no longer serve me (because I can).'

And while you're about it, say,

'I now relinquish everything and everyone in my life that no longer serve me – I let them go with love and good grace.'

But if letting go of the past – along with all it contains that no longer works for you – makes you afraid, try saying:

'As soon as I let go of what no longer serves me, something or someone instantaneously appears to serve me better.'

And if you find that a bit self-centred, say:

'I now serve my comrades, sisters and brothers with love and good grace at all times – the better I serve, the better I am served.'

But going back an affirmation here, this business of manifesting things instantaneously is worthy of a bit of chat.

As in, everything you want eventually manifests instantaneously, though it can often take quite a passage of moments in linear time for that point to be reached. Doublethink, perhaps, in fact almost definitely; however, it does give you a nice kick in the central brain region to affirm something happening instantaneously – and occasionally, especially when affirming general qualities as in most of the above affirmations, results do, in fact, occur instantaneously and on the spot.

Could I just rewind a little way here to return to the idea of feeling exhilarated all the time, as in:

'It's perfectly OK for me to feel exhilarated all the time.'

Because from careful observation over the decades of myself and others, it appears we inhibit our natural exhilaration – we hide it under a cloak of nonchalance, anxiety, depression, stress and other negative states – and were we not to do so, we would actually feel utterly exhilarated all the time, simply for being alive on a planet hurtling through space at 66,000 miles an hour, while spinning on its own axis at 1,000 miles per hour, going goodness knows where. Exhilaration is the natural response to that. And while you may think, 'So what?', 'so what?' is that feeling exhilarated all the time is a hell of a lot more pleasant than feeling stressed, depressed, anxious, nonchalant or any other negative cloaking state you care to mention. And it really is a choice you make, feeling one or the other, no matter how furiously your mind identifies with being depressed, stressed or whatever. But it doesn't matter if you believe me or not – just try saying it for yourself enough times for a moment of exhilaration to surface in your mind, and you'll get enough of a glimpse to see what I'm saying:

'It's perfectly OK for me to feel exhilarated all the time.'

Likewise with your health, which after all is pretty fundamental to enjoying yourself and being active on the path of getting what you want – your good health is also a choice you make. For a start, health feeling exhilarated all the time is a hell of a lot more pleasant than feeling stressed, depressed, anxious, nonchalant or any other negative cloaking state you care to mention.

is only relative – everyone's got something wrong – it's just a matter of managing the health you do enjoy properly enough to sustain and possibly increase it, which can at least be initially effected by affirming such things as:

'It's perfectly OK for me to feel healthy all the time'

or,

'I choose to feel healthy all the time now'

or,

'All the cells of my body are even now being repro-grammed by my unconscious mind to be totally healthy and well.'

And,

'I now enjoy robust health, stamina and vitality all the time.'

But if that provokes a superstitious reaction from within, as if tempting the devil, say:

'I no longer need fear ill-health – health is a choice I make and I choose great, glowing health here and now.'

You can also specify health by body parts, as in:

'I choose health for my liver now, I choose health for my spleen, I choose health for my lungs, I choose health for my heart, I choose health for my brain and nervous system, I choose health for my bones and muscles, I choose health for my sexual organs, I choose health for my bowels, I choose health for my limbs, I choose health for my teeth and gums, I choose health for every other bit of me – what a healthy being am I.'

It's the same with stamina and endurance because you need a lot of each to sustain yourself on the path. Repeat at will:

'I choose to access endless stamina and endurance now to see me through the long haul.'

Accessing is a good device to play with in general, as in:

'I now access limitless health, stamina, vitality, endurance, energy, flexibility, suppleness, vibrancy, vigour and vim.'

Or on a more psycho-emotional level:

'I now access unshakable centredness, calm, serenity, wisdom, perspective, groundedness, rootedness, clarity, concentration, focus and general magnificence, no matter what.'

And talking of no matter what, try:

'I am the queen (or king) of no matter what.'

This phrase comes from a story told me by an old guy called Donovan who is dead now, which goes something like this:

Long ago, once upon a time, there was an ancient kingdom, where all was not so good. The water table level had dropped so low that all the wells had run dry and the people were not only thirsty and miserable but damn smelly too and not a vase of cut flowers was to be seen anywhere in the land.

There was, however, a vast reservoir of fresh water up in the nearby mountains, the contents of which would be easily conductable to the drought-ridden land, except for the fact that the only way up there was via a very thin and dangerous mountain path guarded by the most unwilling to help and hideous hag ever born, who was credited with such magical power and destructive strength that only the strongest warrior

151

could even attempt to challenge her and then only at his (or her, if you must) peril.

So the old king called together all his most valiant knights and sent the most courageous and strong up the mountain. By and by he arrived at the place where the hag stood guard and dismounting his horse suddenly found himself face to face with the ugliest, scariest-looking creature he'd ever seen, complete with huge warts on her nose, long grey hairs growing from her chin and the breath of a thousand sick dogs, not to mention the thick encrusted dirt, pus and other unmentionable dried fluids on all exposed body surfaces.

'If you wish to pass, you must kiss me!' she croaked menacingly, with a mad glint in her eye.

'I will not kiss thee, old hag, stand aside and let me pass!' he valiantly but stupidly replied; and just as he was about to unsheath his mighty sword to slay her, she fixed him with a dreadful and immobilizing stare and all at once grabbed him by the shoulders and threw him clean off the path and into the deep ravine below, where he was dashed upon the rocks and killed.

When he didn't return, the king sent out his second most valiant knight, who suffered exactly the same fate, and finally a third. When he didn't return either, the king fell into a state of great despondency, as did all his courtiers and subjects.

At length, a small voice piped up, 'I will go your majesty and will return victorious!'

The king and all his court turned to see whence the voice had come and there in the middle of the crowd was a young lad with his cap in hand. 'I will go your majesty,' he repeated. The king was just about to say 'Don't be so silly young man, if my three most valiant knights were defeated in the quest, how could you possibly imagine you'd be victorious?,' when he suddenly realized that things were so dire he had nothing to lose.

'OK, young fellow – go with Godspeed!'

So the young man set off up the mountain path and, by and by, he reached the spot where the horrific old hag stood on guard.

'If you will pass by me, young man, you must kiss me,' she croaked.

The young man opened wide his arms and without hesitation replied, 'Not only will I kiss thee, I will embrace thee too!' at which he wrapped the foul hag in his tender arms and kissed her full on the lips.

And no sooner had he done so than she instanta-neously transformed into the most beautiful young princess ever beheld by human eyes.

'You are now the king of no matter what,' she said, gesturing at all the lands that lay below, 'and if you'll have me, I'll be your queen for ever more.'

At which the happy couple returned to the old king, though not before they'd turned on the water supply to the kingdom. The king almost died of joy to see his long-lost daughter, who'd been turned into an old hag by a wicked witch when she was a baby, immediately gave his consent to their happy union and made them king and queen of the realm.

While there are many morals in this little tale, the one that's relevant here is that as soon as you surrender to what's going on, no matter how ugly it may appear, as soon as you accept and embrace it, it immediately transforms into something of great beauty and bounty and you become king or queen of no matter what.

Which isn't half a long way round of saying,

'I am the queen (or king) of no matter what.'

I am the queen (or king) of
no matter what.

Next time you find yourself facing an ugly mess say it and enjoy its transformative effects for yourself.

But let's leave all that for now and turn our attention to making affirmations to manifest specific things or events in real time, without effort or strain, in an enjoyable quantum leap, or series of quantum leaps, as swiftly as possible.

I say 'quantum leap' because *wu wei* makes things happen on the quantum level of reality rather than incrementally in linear fashion, which is exactly why it often looks like nothing's happening. Then all of a sudden you find yourself in a wholly different reality complete with all the things you've visualized – remember, when you affirm things you're simultaneously triggering the associated visualization.

So say, for example, you wanted to manifest a situation where you brought all your talents and skills to bear on doing a job or project that fulfils you creatively and in every other way, and also rewards you with a huge income, try affirming:

'I now manifest the perfect working project for myself, which enables me to use all my talents and skills, including ones I didn't even know I had, easily, effortlessly, enjoyably, swiftly and miraculously in one huge quantum jump.'

remember, you already have what you want here and now, even if you don't like the way it looks.

or, if you wanted to manifest the perfect home for you (and family where relevant) – even if you can't see where the money's coming from, say:

'I now manifest the perfect home for me – even if I can't see where the money's coming from – easily, effortlessly, enjoyably, swiftly and miraculously.'

Obviously, you'll be wise to expect a slight delay before you see the results of this, as it's always tricky finding a perfect home whichever way you cut it, but this delay will be made far easier to handle when you acknowledge that where you live now, even if that's nowhere, is the perfect home for you for now – remember, you already have what you want here and now, even if you don't like the way it looks. Hence,

'By accepting where I am as being exactly where I want to be, I instantaneously trigger a transformative process that brings me to my perfect home, easily, effortlessly, enjoyably, swiftly and miraculously now.'

Or what if you wanted to find yourself involved in the perfect love relationship for you now? Try,

'I now manifest the perfect love relationship for me now, easily, effortlessly, enjoyably, swiftly and miraculously'

I now manifest the perfect love relationship for me now, instantaneously, easily, effortlessly, enjoyably and miraculously.

or if you're really impatient,

'I now manifest the perfect love relationship for me now, instantaneously, easily, effortlessly, enjoyably and miraculously.'

Resist placing any specific person in the picture, as that would constitute bad magic, which will backfire on you – attempting to manipulate specific people through the power of your mind is a misuse of energy. Instead, allow yourself to magnetize whoever it is the Universal Dinner Lady reckons is best, and she'll know because all possible applicants put their relationship requests into her first, whether they realize it or not. Oh, yes, did I mention that she moonlights as the director of the universal dating agency, nights, week-ends and during school breaks? (Well, you can't earn much of a living as a straight ahead dinner lady these days, so who can blame her?)

By the way, it also helps, in this instant, to open your arms in an embracing posture and silently call out to the spirit of the one you're magnetizing into your orbit (even though you have no clue as to their actual identity or whereabouts, you can be certain of the fact that at this very moment in time they do have an identity and are located somewhere on the planet, unless of course you're about to hook up with a nameless extraterrestrial), saying, 'Come – I welcome

open your arms in an
embracing posture and
silently call out to the spirit
of the one you're magnetizing into your orbit, 'come –
I welcome you into my orbit
– I'm ready for you, come
now (if you want)!'

you into my orbit – I'm ready for you, come now (if you want)!' But you really have to feel it – feel the psychic connection occurring, feel them feeling it too and, if you do it with sensitivity, confidence and positive expectations, it can be quite a romantic moment, in a psychic kind of way. But that's not an affirmation, that's an actual beckoning, so back to affirmation city.

Or let's say you want to manifest a sudden fortune of personal wealth of such huge proportions you'd hard-ly know where to put it all, say:

'Easily, effortlessly, enjoyably, swiftly and miracu-lously, I now manifest a sudden fortune of personal wealth of such huge proportions I hardly know where to put it all.'

I use these four examples because those are the four things people generally want most – to be doing work they love that pays them handsomely, to be living in a beautiful home of their own, to be involved in a rela-tionship that hits the spot in every way and to amass a great personal fortune; but of course you can use affirmations for manifesting anything and everything on your list, from the most trivial and banal to the most magnificent and meaningful. It can, for instance, be nothing more (or less) significant than cleaning the bathroom and putting the dirty towels in the washing machine when you're really not in the mood but really

have to, because there are no clean towels, the bathroom is disgusting and you need to take a shower, in
which case, say,

**'I now clean the bathroom and put all the dirty tow-
els in the washing machine in good time to dry them
so I can take a shower and get out of here in time to
do what I have to do later, easily, effortlessly, enjoyably, and miraculously.'**

You may think it stupid to use your magical powers in
such mundane matters, but it's better than sitting
around like a lazy, unwashed lump getting depressed
about it – and yes, people do get depressed over silly
things like that.

But you know what, unless I think of some specific
things to use as examples of stuff you may like to
manifest by affirmation, in which case I'll insert them
later so seamlessly you won't even notice (probably
just before this particular sentence in fact, so you'll
never see the join – that's magic for you), I fancy stopping that particular stream of thought here, and wind-
ing up this affirmation session with some grand catch-
all declarations that make all the other affirmations
come alive. And it's important to stop doing affirmations when you get bored or they lose their freshness
– never labour over them, in other words, but always
let making them up be a thing of joy. So saying, say:

it's important to stop doing affirmations when you get bored or they lose their freshness – never labour over them and always let making them up be a thing of joy.

'Making up affirmations is a thing of joy for me, and the more joy I evoke in myself, the more swiftly I manifest what I want.'

Then,

'I find myself utterly delightful in all my dealings with others.'

This because, as previously pointed out, most of what you want to get for yourself in the world comes to you through other people – the Dinner Lady sends, but it's the people who deliver – therefore it's desirable for you to like the way you interact, because if you like it, others will too.

And,

'I now open myself to receive happy and willing cooperation from others'

or,

'I now inspire happy and willing cooperation from others'

and,

'I am always in the right place at the right time, with the right people, doing the right thing with the right result (for me and them, at this time)'

and

'The Universal Dinner Lady loves me and brings me everything I need now.'

Of course, substitute Dinner Lady for any other mon-icker for the divine you care to employ, and say:

'My concept of the divine supports me now'

and,

'I have the power to manifest everything I want, in the appropriate way for me for now, in accord with the free will of everyone involved and in line with what's for their highest possible good and mine – and that's exactly what I do.'

'I create my own reality'

and say it again:

'I create my own reality'

and again:

the Universal Dinner Lady
loves me and brings me
everything I need.

'I create my own reality'

and so on ...

'I create my own reality'
'I create my own reality'
'I create my own reality'
'I create my own reality'
'I create my own reality'
'I create my own reality'
'I create my own reality'
'I create my own reality'
'I create my own reality'
'I create my own reality'
'I create my own reality.'

Then finally, close off the session with a closing-off phrase of your choice along the lines of,

'So be it'

or,

'So let it be'

or,

'Let it be so'

or,

'Aye, it is so'

or simply,

'Over to you now, Dinner Lady.'

issuing invitations to the spirits

As we touched on just now, as well as affirming this or that, you're also perfectly at liberty to speak, so to speak, directly to the essence or spirit of something and invite it into your orbit and, while doing this may constitute nothing more than unbridled indulgence in play acting, it can trigger positive results if you're in the mood for it. So say, for example, you feel you need unshakable confidence to help you through a particular phase of activity or to help you through the rest of your life in general, address the *a priori* essence or 'spirit' of unshakable confidence and say,

'Spirit of unshakable confidence, I welcome you into my life now – come, come'

or,

'Spirit of unshakable confidence, enter me now.'

And if you want success,

**'Spirit of success, I welcome you into my life now –
come, come'**

or,

'Spirit of success, enter me now'

or even,

'Enter me now, spirit of success.'

Of course, you can phrase it how you like. So if you
wanted wealth, you could even say:

'Spirit of wealth, be in me now'

or,

**'I welcome you into my life now, spirit of wealth,
come, come, come.'**

It obviously doesn't matter as long as you feel yourself
making connection with the essence of whatever you wish
to invite into your life at this time and it can be applied to
anything you want – abundance, love, popularity, health,

tranquility, wisdom, enlightenment, joy, courage, beauty, sexiness – you name it, you can invite it in.

It also helps to visualize it entering you through the pores of your skin and filling you, perhaps as a vapour or light, perhaps as a big, huge spirit with a brightly coloured tutu – again, it really doesn't matter as long as you engage with it from the depths of your being. It's the equivalent of what those in the occult idiom call invoking, which can be potent, but only when you're in the mood – otherwise it's just plain weird.

going for essence

This works well at those times you are overcome by longing – usually for someone you love or think you love, or even just fancy, and it goes like this. You imagine how it would make you feel being with that person right now – let's make it up – you'd probably feel warm, safe, desirable, valued, validated, acknowledged, excited, entertained, sexy and altogether wonderful. So you affirm something like,

'I now access warmth from within'

and you'd 'feel' that warmth spreading throughout your body and especially round your heart, as that's where you'd feel it most if you were with the object of your longing.

Then you say:

'I choose to feel safe now'

or simply,

'I am safe'

and you allow yourself to relax and feel safe here and now, then:

'I am desirable'

'I value myself'

'I validate myself now'

'I acknowledge myself now'

'I excite myself now'

and I don't mean like that, you saucy thing, though it can be like that if you want. Then,

'I allow myself to be fully entertained by life here and now'

I am sexy and altogether
wonderful in every way.

and

'I am sexy and altogether wonderful in every way.'

And if you really mean those things when you say them, or at least method act like you mean them, not only will you significantly reduce the longing, thus regaining your personal power and equipoise to some extent but, more importantly, you will also trigger a change in the vibrational quality of your energy field that will draw someone from the world around you – maybe the person you long for, maybe someone even more appropriate – to come and join you in the fun. Because that's how it works. When you're feeling needy, it triggers a negative reaction in your energy field, which repulses rather than attracts. As soon as you even acknowledge the possibility you can satisfy that need by yourself, it raises your vibrational rate and people are drawn to you. In other words, no one wants to eat in an empty restaurant.

And this applies, not only to when you long for a person but when you long for anything. So say you find yourself longing for your perfect house, you imagine the feelings that would give you, were you to be living in it here and now – let's make it up – say, secure, comfortable, successful, calm and delighted. Then you make up affirmations, do an invocation, visualize, or do all three, to the effect that you access

when you're feeling needy,
it triggers a negative reaction in your energy field
which repulses rather than
attracts.

and experience a moment of security, comfort, success, calm and delight. That way you reduce the longing and thus regain equilibrium – and remember, the Dinner Lady won't dance with you in a state of disequilibrium – and before you know it, she'll be knocking on your door with the keys, deeds and instructions for the washing machine and electric garage door in her hand – and maybe even the tweezers too.

But, of course, it's the regaining of balance in the moment, here and now, that's most important – not the getting of your object of desire, because here and now is all there is. As soon as balance returns, you look around and say, 'I have manifested all this, because this is exactly what I want, even if it's a bit of a mess sometimes – clever me.' In other words, you make peace with your reality again, which is ultimately what it's all about (if it's all about anything at all, that is).

wishing

Again, it's a matter of taste and mood. If you find yourself in the mood for making wishes, then it's probably best to start by wishing for everything to be exactly as it is. This is the equivalent of acknowledging that you have exactly what you want already, which puts you in a position of (personal) power and, what's more, you get an instant result, which is good for your confidence.

Wishing is a bit of a mystical business at best – a bit like an only partly formed visualization or affirmation that implies you don't fully trust your own power to manifest (things) – but that's fine when you're in the mood, as I say.

Wishing is really telling the Dinner Lady what to put on your plate, so you might want to visualize her listening to you when you make a wish – it doesn't matter – some people throw coins in wishing wells, some light candles in churches, others like to superimpose an image of what they want on the face of the full moon, with the idea that their wish will be made manifest by the next full moon. Myself, when I used to live at the Highgate Egg, everytime I walked home from the clinic (I was treating people then as my day job), I'd pass through Waterlow Park, pass beneath the arch at the end of one of the old walled gardens and say, 'As I pass beneath this arch, I leave the past behind me and enter into an entirely new world complete with everything I want,' at which point, if feeling particularly mentally muscular, I would pause for a moment and list all the things I wanted, which (along with everything else) seems to have worked a treat.

the more you reinforce your vision, the better, providing you don't fall prey to obsessing over it.

But that was just my little ritual. I'm sure you already have a ritual repertoire of your own, but if not, allow yourself to invent a little something to use at such times. Essentially, the more you reinforce your vision, the better, providing you don't fall prey to obsessing over it. But we'll talk about that later. For now, make a wish. Why not?

praying

Sometimes people like to pray. Some people like to pray all the time. Some people pray to this, some to that. Some embellish their prayers with special prayer words, which they invest with special prayer power, some people pray using no words at all, allowing their hearts to do the talking instead. Some people pray in a dedicated house of prayer according to which, if any, religion they buy into, others pray in an airplane toilet, say when caught midstream with their pants down in sudden, unexpectedly severe turbulence. Some pray to a male god, some to a female, some even pray to the Dinner Lady.

The point is, whether you pray this way or that or not at all, it is good to remain in a prayerful state, meaning a continual state of awareness of the fact that you're dancing with the Tao, the divine, or yes, the Universal

Dinner Lady, because maintaining this state is what gives your vision – your life, in other words – substance and meaning. In actual fact, all the preceding text so far constitutes training in prayerfulness – I mention this only in case you're a praying kind of guy (or girl), but it's only another way of framing the same picture, so don't get too hung up on it, unless of course you enjoy getting hung up. Perhaps far more important is the ability to engage in the following.

breathing love into (your picture of) everyone and everything

Nothing like it – a bit of love breathed into everyone and everything, or at least your picture of everyone and everything, does wonders every time. Try it now. Start by picturing those closest to you as you inhale. As you exhale, visualize a stream of love (pink vapour if you like), issuing forth from the centre of your chest and engulfing them in pleasant ways – see them get it too. Then picture all the people you work with, one by one or grouped in a crowd scene, and do likewise. Then picture anyone you may be having difficulty with and give them double portions (of love, not difficulty). This of course can include people you don't actually know – perhaps people in the news whose actions perturb you, or can indeed include the entire human

breathe love to everyone
in the whole world – don't
bother with the one by
one scenario – a simple
massive crowd scene will
do.

race if you're finding them all a tad tricky to manage. In any case, breathe love to everyone in the whole world – don't bother with the one by one scenario – a simple massive crowd scene will do. And don't stop there. Breathe love into every animal, bird, fish, insect, spider, tree, plant, flower, blade of grass, rock, mountain, stream, ocean – and don't forget the buildings, sewage systems, phonelines, planes, cars, boats, trains and general infrastructure because they need love too – and then even the moon, the sun, the planets, stars, asteroids, comets, black holes – yes even them – and eventually the entire universe. And while you're about it, breathe love into your projects, your relationships and anything and everything that comprises your life, including you, your body, your mind, your clothes, your hair, skin and bath products, your tweezers, your food, your fluid, your house, your car and even your yellow leopard skin hat, if you have one.

Indeed, you'll soon notice that pretty much as soon as you've done a love-breathing session, amazing things start happening, not least of which is you feeling extremely pleasant (and loving). Try it. It's a lovely way to make miracles happen, literally.

miracles?

Making wine out of water – or if you've a feel for market trends and an eye on the main chance, water out of wine – is obviously a metaphor for transforming one set of circumstances into another more useful one in one fair swoop of a quantum jump. Not that I'm saying with the right training in this life or previous ones you couldn't actually transform one fluid into another (without it passing through your bladder that is), but that's not the point. The point is to be aware that reality actually occurs on the quantum plane. The linear plane, where things seem to happen incrementally along a timeline stretching into the so-called future, is merely an illusory device we conjure between us to enable us to make sense of it all. Whereas, when you've got your eyes straight, you soon realize it's all actually happening at once in a lateral field of limitless possibilities with you in the centre of an endless series of concentric circles of exponentially increasing size. And if, in any particular moment, you happen to be whatever it is you have to be to cut through the illusion with enough focus and clarity, you can materialize wine out of water, water out of wine or even washing-up liquid out of old bits of carpet if that's what sings your song for you. But it is, as is everything on the linear plane, merely a trick of the light and, hence, a miracle (which literally means trick of the light), though if you want to be more precise, call it a quantum event – it sounds less nonsey.

so, can you actually change your destiny doing all this stuff? (the destiny vs free will question)

I don't know. No one ever has known, no one does and no one ever will, unless they're a hell of a lot cleverer than wot I am, or you for that matter. It's an imponderable. Indeed, pondering it is a classic example of intellectual masturbation – a complete waste of energy and time. Leave that to Dr Squid Gridlo and the other philosophers of this world.

You can certainly manifest what you want, but then wasn't that what your destiny dictated you'd do? Does it matter? If you want to think you can actually change your destiny, then think it. If that scares or troubles you, then don't. It makes no difference whatsoever. The main thing is to optimize your life in all its aspects, especially the enjoyment of it, while you still have a life to optimize, by manifesting whatever it is you want. When you're just about to drop your body and cross over into the other realm, you can look back and say, 'Ah, so that was my destiny!'

as soon as you've done a love-breathing session, amazing things start happening.

But to try and define it ahead of time is merely a game for fools. It's fine not to know. That's a damn good affirmation, by the way, 'It's fine for me not to know.' Because we're all so busy trying to know things, when we more or less know very little at all considering the scope and scale of this universe – so give knowing a break for a while. And talking of not knowing, can you tell the difference between the following?

wanting and needing

Because I'm not sure I can. Obviously what you need are the first few basic requirements mentioned in the original want-list visualization template – air, water, food, shelter, clothing, human warmth, health and, I suppose, sex from time to time – I say suppose because there are many celibate nuns, monks and other assorted holy people who don't.

Beyond that list, we're into the realm of embellishment – entertainment, love, better sex, more sex, wealth, intellectual development, status, popularity, travel, vehicles, equipment, status symbols, excitement, acknowledgement in one form or another, adventure (an advanced form of entertainment), spiritual clarity, sense of purpose – I'm just reeling them out here but you can complete your own list.

don't worry about whether
you need or want some-
thing – if you want it, see
it as yours and it will be,
in the form and manner
you need.

So you could be tempted to delineate between the two and call the basic needs, needs and the embellishments, wants. But that doesn't take into account how, from a larger perspective, your overall healthy growth as an individual may well need entertainment, perhaps to stimulate creativity; may well need adventure to push you beyond your comfort limits and may well need some really fancy clothes to go to a really fancy do you've been invited to – who knows? I don't.

So while it's possible to draw a distinction between needing a good hug and wanting one, it's probably a bit of a moot point.

I only mention all this in case you think you should only be concerned with manifesting things you need rather than want, as if this will endear you more to the Universal Dinner Lady (which in fact it won't, so don't bother). She loves to give you what you need and will do so as long as you allow her, and that will also include what you want, but in a form and manner you need for your overall healthy growth as an individual. In other words, don't worry about whether you need or want something – if you want it, see it as yours and it will be, in the form and manner you need.

But surely, isn't it ...

wrong to manifest things in an era of rapidly dwindling resources?

Well, it's not really a question of right or wrong. People have been going about the business of getting what they want since people were first seen wandering about the planet and will continue to do so until there are none left to be seen. That's the basic drive of nature programmed into our deepest circuitry. And it's that same drive, to progress along the path in more and more efficient, comfortable and enjoyable ways, that has not only led to the oil and nuclear age, during which consumerism reached its apotheosis, but also, more crucially to this, the dawning of the solar age, during which genuinely sustainable energy sources will be sufficiently commercially developed to supply all the world's needs. Along with this, developing in parallel, is the technology and know-how to grow genuinely sustainable crops, to optimize the use of recycling methods and generally produce everything we need in a far more intelligent and eco-friendly fashion.

Bear in mind that these new technologies, on which our survival as a species *en masse* will fully depend, have not been developed in the main by altruistic holy men and women, but by people driven by the entrepreneurial spirit – the drive, in other words, to get what they want. Do I need to spell out the case for getting what you want any further?

it's about getting what
you want in an intelligent,
aware manner, rather
than simply plundering
what's available without
conscience.

It's about getting what you want in an intelligent, aware manner, rather than simply plundering what's available without conscience. It's about attaining true quality in your life and all its aspects rather than following the false allure of attaining huge quantity. In all, it's actually impossible to stop wanting. The only way you can stop wanting something is to get it – or get something even better. Best thing is to go with that force, that primal urge to improve, for from that will spring the technology that will save us.

Realizing that, you'll probably be thinking, 'Oh come on then, let's hurry up because there really isn't much time left the way we're going,' which is exactly why it's so useful to avail yourself of the following technique whenever required.

stretching and shrinking time

Time itself is merely a contruct, a device; an idea we believe in to help us make order of an unorderable reality. Time, therefore, as any ancient Taoist or Einstein you'd care to ask will tell you, is not real but relative.

You can't control the speed the planet's travelling at through space, but you can take full command of your perception of how long it takes to pass through, say, one day and night's worth of 24 hours. Hence, when faced with such a gargantuan task as saving the world of humans from its own destruction by the creation and development of sustainable technologies, energy sources and ultimately ideologies, one working in the field in any way (and that includes you, directly or indi-rectly), would wish to stretch time in relation to that particular endeavour.

If, on the other hand, you found yourself obliged to spend 24 hours in the company of someone you found intensely boring, irritating and generally wearing to be with, you'd wish to shrink time in relation to that particular obligation. In neither case would you be shrinking or stretching time itself – but your perception of it and only in relation to the case in question. So, when stretching it to give yourself more chance of sav-ing the world while it's still possible, you'll only be stretching it as far as that particular project goes. It won't mean that every time you sit on the loo the ses-sion will feel like it's lasting hours (unless you do actu-ally spend hours sitting there, of course, which is a silly thing to do, so stop it now). By the same token, if you shrink time for the purposes of getting through an unwelcome obligation as painlessly as possible, you'll only be shrinking time in relation to that. Standing at the checkout in the supermarket, you'll still have the same time you usually do to get your money out, pay

you can take full command
of your perception of how
long it takes to pass
through one day and
night's worth of 24 hours.
time is not real, but
relative.

for your food, stick it in bags and stick the bags back on the trolley. Unless you're that person who often manages to be in the queue in front of me, fumbling about for 31p for what seems like forever, in which case, get a move on will you – you're holding everyone up.

And the way you do it is as simple as this. You encapsulate the time frame involved, as it relates to the task, obligation, or indeed intended pleasurable interlude in and, addressing the Dinner Lady, say,

'Shrink the time, Dinner Lady'

or

'Stretch the time, Dinner Lady',

as required, not imperiously but in a similar (suggestive) tone to that you'd use if saying, 'Go on, make us a cup of tea while you're up.'

And it will happen. Remember, what you're really doing is stretching or shrinking your perception of that passage of time, only as it relates to a particular set of circumstances. And talking of time ...

mouth (in case you suddenly lose control and start biting it), and arms held out in front, as if clasping a large vertical roll of silk to your chest, which prevents your two hands, whose palms are facing your chest, from meeting by about the width of a large pomegranate. Keep your arms well rounded and unlocked at the elbows and wrists. Breathe freely and allow all the muscles of your body to sink groundwards, while trusting in your skeletal structure to maintain your person in the upright position, perpendicular to the ground. Slowly turn your palms outwards and push through the air to the sides as if swimming breaststroke, holding your arms out to the sides without pulling back on your shoulder joints. Keep breathing freely and relaxing your muscles.

Your palms should now be facing away from you to the sides. In this position, say to yourself, the Tao, the Dinner Lady, or anyone who cares to listen,

'I now release the past along with everyone and everything that needs to be set free, as well as all negativity, anxiety, stress, self-recrimination, self-limitation, suffering, pain and doubt.'

And feel yourself releasing it through the centre of each palm on every exhalation. It may take a few, so keep your shoulders and neck relaxed in the posture and trust your legs to support you.

I now release the past,
along with everyone and
everything that needs to be
set free.

When you feel you've released enough for one day, slowly turn your palms to face towards you, with your arms still in the wide-open embrace position, and say (to yourself, the Tao, the Dinner Lady or anyone who cares to listen):

'I now welcome the new into my life and, with it, everyone and everything I need, to manifest what I want, along with beauty, warmth, health, strength, vitality, longevity, security, excitement, wealth, adventure, travel – and indeed anything and everything I want in my life right now.'

And as you inhale, feel yourself receiving the essence or spirit of all that into your person through the palms of your hands. This will also take a few moments, so continue to relax your neck and shoulders and to keep breathing freely. Finally, when you've taken in enough for one day, slowly return your arms to the front and turn your palms in to face your chest again, at which point declare, 'Aye, it is so!' or words of your own choosing to that effect. This is one way to keep your mind disciplined enough on an ongoing basis to avoid various pitfalls such as ...

obsessing over getting what you want

Has there ever been a time in your life when you found yourself totally obsessed with someone as a potential or actual love object? Conversely, has there ever been a time when you were the object of someone's obsession?

If there has been either or both and there probably has, if you're old enough to be reading this manifesto, by dint of being interested in getting what you want, then you'll be aware of how utterly, horribly unattractive that is from the point of view of the object of the obsession. And it just makes the object of obsession, whether it's you or the other, want to run away as quickly as possible. Well, the same goes for anything you want, whether you're talking about a quality, a possession or group of possessions, or an event or events involving various other people. If you obsess about it, it wants to run away from you as swiftly as it can.

But how to stop yourself when it's something you really, really, really want? Firstly, by remaining aware. Aware specifically of dancing with the Dinner Lady, which is what you're doing here – manifesting being your Tao or Zen (your path and focus), rather than the actual results. As soon as you lose awareness of

if you obsess about
something, it wants to run
away from you as swiftly
as it can.

enjoying the dance and focus instead on the results you hope to achieve from it, you've come off the path and need to regroup. Otherwise you do fall into an obsessive state which delays the process because you're too much in the way for what you want to get through.

Secondly, you train yourself to enter a meditative state wherein you find yourself momentarily unattached to the desire or the object of desire, whether that be a new house and swimming pool or a deeply passionate love affair, or indeed both – why not?

This can be achieved at the deepest level by reading and learning the Taoist meditation system from *Return of the Urban Warrior – High Speed Spirituality for People on the Run* by this very same author, who can explain it to you far better than I. (And that's not even a plug, but if you have taken the trouble and time to write a succinct manual on the subject for the express purpose of making the information clearly available and accessible to busy people with busy lives, why shouldn't you take advantage of that fact to let them know?)

Meantime, it's really just a simple matter of learning to relax your body, slow down and regulate your breathing, elongate your spine, broaden your shoulders and hips, whether sitting, standing, lying down and

as soon as you lose awareness of enjoying the dance
and focus instead on the
results you hope to achieve
from it, you've come off the
path.

eventually while on the move, and drawing your point of local awareness back into the centre of your brain – maintaining it there at all times for the rest of your life, whether at work, rest or play. Like this it's almost impossible to get stuck on an obsession for long, as it becomes too physically and psychically uncomfortable to sustain.

However, if you fear you're in danger of becoming obsessed by something you want badly, or indeed you already are obsessed, you might want to consider either taking a pleasant vacation in the sun to get yourself to ease off a bit or to repeat something along the lines of the following affirmation with some frequency,

'I now breathe, relax and relinquish all obsessive tendencies towards the objects of my desire and, as I do, the objects of my desire stop being so elusive and, by and by, come closer and closer into my orbit of themselves.'

And talking of more affirmations …

affirmation city overspill

You can never do enough affirmations – it's a constant challenge to maintain supremacy of the positive urge over the negative default mode within. Which is probably a rationalization for the fact that I feel like writing a few more affirmations right now, specifically rabble-rousing, multi-sentence affirmations, and wondered if you'd care to join me.

Actually, that's not strictly true – I was really planning to introduce rabble-rousing multi-sentence affirmations at this very point for your sake, but you know when you're sitting all alone writing a book, you could swear there's someone there reading it as you go, as if you're talking to someone – in this case, you – but there isn't someone there at all, in fact (at least at the time of writing), so it's not a lie either. And I do feel like writing some anyway, even though there's a big part of me – the six-year-old part – who would absolutely love to trundle down to the beach now and play in the sun. But enough video diary from the author telling the story of writing the book. Back to you.

So how about ...

you can never do enough
affirmations.

'I now move as a unified whole, with all parts of me, including my inner six-year-old, as well as all the other parts, acting in unison. Like this, I am focused and concentrated and nothing can stand in my way of achieving what I want now, not even me.'

And,

'I have supreme confidence when I choose to access it and I choose to access it now. With supreme confidence I can achieve anything I want, which is exactly what I'm doing here and now'

or,

'I am imbued with infinite courage, with infinite courage, I am imbued. Imbued with infinite courage, no challenge, however scary or daunting, is too great for me to take on successfully.'

And,

'My mind is rooted in the creative hub of the universe. My body is fuelled by the generative force at the creative hub of the universe. With my mind rooted and my body fuelled by the very hub of the universe, there is nothing I can't achieve'

or,

I have supreme confidence when I choose to access it and I choose to access it now. with supreme confidence I can achieve anything I want, which is exactly what I'm doing here and now.

'I have the vision, strength, fortitude, endurance, follow-through, clarity, focus, determination, dedication, wisdom, compassion, health, resources and support to achieve anything and everything I want now. I now unleash myself on the path.'

And,

'I am unique. I have a unique gift to bring my world. I now give my world my unique gift and my world rewards me with wealth, success, love and deep, lasting pleasure.'

'I am free to do whatever I choose. I have everything to gain and nothing to lose.'

And (just in case you go a bit psycho with the power of it all),

'My choices are wise, life-promoting and rooted in deep compassion for myself and everyone. I know exactly which way to go, moment by moment, and my path leads from scenes of splendour to greater splendour with every step I take.'

my choices are wise,
life-promoting and rooted
in deep compassion for
myself and everyone.

'Even when it looks to me like I'm messing things up, I am in fact always on the right path, doing the right thing, in the right way, with the right result for everyone. And even if I don't believe that some-times, it's true.'

And,

'I am pure love in motion. Wherever I go, people just want to smile and laugh with glee without even knowing why. Every situation I step into is already healed and repaired by my very presence. I am pure love in motion.'

And,

'It's fine for me to acknowledge myself. The more I acknowledge myself, the stronger my positive qual-ities grow now. Indeed, I am confident, damn sexy, irresistible, successful and altogether magnificent. Even if I do say so myself.'

And that is true, even if I do say so myself.

Or what about,

'With every breath I take, with ever step I make, I grow stronger, healthier, more youthful, more beau-tiful, more confident, more successful, richer, more loving, more loved, wiser, more compassionate, more focused, clearer, sexier, more flexible, more adaptable and more intelligent. This is happening now, even when I think I'm messing things up. I really am one hell of a guy (or girl).'

'Everything is possible now. Behind the scenes, the Dinner Lady is making many wonderful things ready to manifest. Incredible things are happening right now.'

Is your rabble roused? Do you feel sufficiently exhorted? If any of those affirmations appeal to your senses or at least don't make you cringe, take any or all of them and write, speak or sing them at least six times each, for while I admit they're by no means the best lyrics I've ever produced, the sentiments they carry are about as good as sentiments get and so are well worth inculcating into your deeper circuitry. But please don't be restricted to simply copying them unless you're happy to do so. Instead, use them over time as a guide to trigger your own lyrics, as this tends to work best in the long run. And talking of long runs, while your long-term (approximately 1008 days) vision may well already be growing stronger by the hour, in the short term, it's inevitable that you'll be beset by doubt and fear; in fact your mental, and hence emotional, state is quite likely to undergo a fair bit of the following.

everything is possible
now. behind the scenes,
the dinner lady is making
many wonderful things
ready to manifest.
incredible things are
happening right now.

swinging between utter confidence and utter fear about four times every hour

If you were under the impression that having a strong vision, backed up by a focused, dedicated mind, precluded the inevitablity of swinging between utter confidence that you can manifest everything you want and utter fear that you won't – about four times evey hour – then allow me to disabuse you of that notion this very instant.

Of course, you get your good days, when nothing short of falling foul of a suicide bomber could shake your poise, but you can't count on them. The variables that contribute to the perceived goodness or badness of any particular day are too many to list, but include such factors as how much sleep you had the night before, how much sleep you had the night before that, and before that; what you ate for dinner last night, the night before that and possibly every night for the preceding three weeks; as well as what you had for lunch and breakfast, how much alcohol you drank last night and so on; how many and what kinds of drugs you took last night, the night before that and so on; how many cigarettes you smoked; the way your partner, lover, children, boss, colleague, hairdresser, acupuncturist, beautician, personal trainer, guru, friend, PR consultant, customer, cleaner, chauffeur, cab driver, flight attendant or unknown stranger in the street looked at you today, yesterday, the day before and so on; the weather today, yesterday and so on; light levels in the sky, season, position of the moon and other planets, solar flare activity levels; childhood memories; stories in the news; state of the economy; share index levels; property prices; oil prices; pollution levels; pollen levels; and whether your shoes and hair look good.

So there's obviously no use reckoning your state of general being against whether it'll be a good day or not. Probably best to reckon on most days swinging out in all directions – good, bad, up, down and side-ways. Probably best to expect yourself to swing inter-nally likewise. The important thing is to identify with that within which observes the swing, rather than with the swinging itself.

You are not the confidence. Neither are you the fear. Who you actually are is too huge to put in words, for you are nothing less than your entire universe, not to mention being the Dinner Lady herself in disguise; so for now, let's just say you're the watcher, the witness, the observer of the play between the confidence and fear, the good and the bad, the god and the devil, the yang and the yin. Don't beat yourself in other words (unless of course you enjoy it, you fruitcake). Instead, calmly, compassionately, tell yourself,

you are not the confidence.
neither are you the fear.
who you actually are is too
huge to put in words, for
you are nothing less than
your entire universe.

'It's OK to swing between pure confidence and utter terror as many times an hour as I like, as long as I find it enjoyable.'

Obviously there's no point engaging in any activity if you're not enjoying it. This doesn't mean you try to avoid activities you think you won't enjoy, even though you know they're actually unavoidable, and divert yourself with any or many of life's distractions. It means relinquishing self-pity enough to accept where you are and what's happening, taking responsibility for having created it, being wise enough to tell yourself to enjoy it no matter how unenjoyable you think it is and being strong enough to follow through in a cheerful manner. So don't let the swing perturb you – relax and enjoy it. It has no bearing on the big picture. Say:

'My vision is strong, so am I, and it makes no difference how much swinging I do in any given hour, my vision is even now being made manifest before my very eyes.'

Either that or phone up a friend and have a moan – that usually does the trick.

my vision is strong, so am I, and it makes no difference how much swinging I do in any given hour, my vision is even now being made manifest before my very eyes.

serving (others) brings sanity

What gets you lost in the darker, more lunatic recess-es of the labyrinth of your mind is forgetting that your function here is to serve, and getting caught up in the belief that getting what you want is something sepa-rate from that. Just like a flower in the garden, whose function is to serve the greater good by looking pretty, providing pollen for bees and adventure playground rides for small insects and fairies, and whose every need is met by the great gardener of life until the great gardener decides to cut it down and sell it to a cut flower wholesaler, you are here to serve the greater good in your own way and all your needs are met like-wise. The only difference is you probably won't end up in someone's vase on a coffee table or mantlepiece.

Remembering your function (to serve) immediately restores your sanity when you've got stuck in some nasty mental loop or other. Remembering to ask, 'How can I serve here?' rather than, 'What can I get here?' is a fundamental key to getting what you want (ironically). And the way you serve best is by enjoying yourself, no matter what – always be the small child laughing in wonder at the unlikelihood of the whole damn game of life. Because like this, you're cheerful, and when you're cheerful, you spread cheer to others. Cheer counters fear. And as fear subsides, people invent and create all manner of wonders to be enjoyed

no greater service can
you do humankind than fill
it with cheer to counter its
fear.

by all. Indeed, no greater service can you do humankind than fill it with cheer to counter its fear. But that doesn't mean you should go into denial about the horrible pain that lurks beneath the surface of every mind. Nor does it mean you should become cynical either.

so, how do you deal with the negative responses your mind throws up to counter your affirmations?

So you're sitting there affirming,

'I remain cheerful now no matter my external conditions and I'm radiating cheer to everyone around'

over and over, and your inner cynic, the hurt young child who didn't resolve the pain of that first inevitable betrayal (by life, mother, father, sibling, teacher, schoolfriend, or whoever), feels obliged to retort, 'Do me a favour – I'm feeling as shit as the cesspits at a summer rock festival and no amount of rah-rah is going to change that fact' or, 'As much as it would be fine and dandy for me to forget all my troubles right now and start wombling about with a big grin on my face, it's hardly likely to happen, is it?' and even, 'This affirmation business is a load of utter bollocks,' for example. You can make up your own negative retorts for yourself and already do, I'm sure – that's easy, anyone can do it.

But what takes more mettle, what separates the heroes from the sheep, is to persevere regardless. You continue to repeat the affirmation (or one of your own and, most probably, more eloquent composition) and to every negative retort from your inner critic, you simply respond, 'Thank you for sharing' or even, 'Thank you for sharing that – your views have been acknowledged and will be considered – I know you're feeling hard done by and afraid but stay with the programme here and I'm sure you'll be happy with the result, because, my friend, I remain cheerful now no matter my external conditions and I'm radiating cheer to everyone around and, in that atmosphere, I manifest everything I want easily, effortlessly, enjoyably, swiftly and miraculously, which makes me even more cheerful and hence able to radiate even more cheer to everyone around me, so everyone wins – including you, you little bastard,' (I mean you say this to your inner critic, not that you're a little bastard – though of course you might be and may continue to be so for as long as you find the results progressive for you).

If the inner critic is still dissatisfied, remind yourself,

acknowledge the negativity
in your mind but choose
to override it by continuing
to reinforce the positive.

'I create my own reality'

and if your inner critic doesn't instantly see the sense in that, borrow from my personal sacred mantra for stilling the thoughts mentioned earlier and say, 'Shut the f*** up!' with the suffix, 'will you?!', as optional.

In short, you acknowledge the negativity in your mind but choose to override it by continuing to reinforce the positive.

And that's how you do it.

developing the will to receive

So you're shuffling along slowly in the school canteen queue, looking at the floor or at the dodgy haircut of the person in front of you, when all of a sudden you find yourself before the Universal Dinner Lady, who's looking sexy, voluptuous and bountiful with her premium brand silk underwear, stockings and heels beneath her pinny; and you're holding out your plate and saying, 'Give me everything, Dinner Lady – I want it all – not just purity of heart or peace of mind, but absolutely everything!' and she looks down at your plate and retorts, 'On that little thing?'

unfettered by self-limiting thoughts, my receptacle is limitless in its capacity to receive the innumerable blessings the Dinner Lady has to bestow.

If you want everything – everything in your vision – the world you desire to manifest for yourself, you realize, as you look down at your plate, you'll have to construct a larger plate – a far larger plate indeed. For now, however, she slops on as much apple pie and custard as your plate will hold and, with drops of custard dripping over the edge, you find yourself somewhere to sit and tuck in.

So how to enlarge your receptacle?

In actual fact, it's not so much a matter of enlarging the receptacle, because unfettered by self-limiting thoughts and their correlating holding patterns in the connective tissue of your body and hence energy field, your receptacle is limitless in its capacity to receive the innumerable blessings the Dinner Lady has to bestow.

In most people, the blocking mechanism tends to be concentrated around the chest region, or heart centre if you want to get spiritual about it. The work of enlargement, therefore, consists in learning to release the muscle armouring around your chest, no doubt mostly unconscious, leaving yourself, as it were, with an open heart. This, of course, makes you vulnerable, which is why you developed the armour in the first place. However, to receive you have to be receptive, hence vulnerable. If you fear being wounded by life by adopting a vulnerable stance, take up a martial art, specifically a Taoist one such as tai chi, hsing i, or pa kua, as these help you develop a protective shield of energy, which is not only far more effective at protecting you from the negative energy of others, but is also good for your health, whereas muscular armouring merely constricts the flow of blood and energy and thereby hastens your demise. Additionally, or alternatively, repeat such affirmations as,

'The more vulnerable I make myself in order to increase my capacity to receive, the safer I am.'

Remember, you create your own reality. Say it (again), go on,

'I create my own reality.'

Along with consciously paying attention to relaxing the muscles of your chest, it really helps to visualize your chest expanding to encompass the entirety of everything in your vision you wish to manifest and more, as if you hold the entire universe of your visualization there comfortably. To close the visualization, compress the vision to the size of a small marble and send it down to your lower abdomen and thence into the loop for nine internal revolutions or so – remember that?

you get stronger the more you carry, but the more you can do to strengthen yourself ahead of the load, the better.

By and by, your will to receive will increase just because you've told it to and the Dinner Lady will always be heaping as much on your plate as it will take. The next thing is to increase the strength of your arms, shoulders, back, legs, and all the rest of you, so you can carry the plate without falling over.

One of the reasons you can initially feel so disorientated and unsettled when you get what you want, and why the old saying goes, 'be careful what you wish for, it might come true,' is because you may not have yet developed the requisite measure of strength to carry or contain it all. Luckily, you get stronger the more you carry but, the more you can do to strengthen yourself ahead of the load, the better. Hence the importance of visualizing yourself strong, of affirming that you're growing stronger by the nanosecond and commanding yourself to be strong. Of course, physical exercise to strengthen your physical body will help enormously, even though what we're on about here is in the realms of the metaphysical. As above, so below. Strengthen the metaphysical aspect and the physical will change in response. Conversely, strengthen the physical and, with the correct intention, the metaphysical will be strengthened likewise. For real, if you sit on a bench pumping free weights and tell yourself by doing so, you're accelerating the materialization of your vision by developing your will to receive, then that's what will happen, because – and by now I'm sure you don't need reminding – you create your own reality.

Finally, it pays to examine and flush out any negative, self-restricting beliefs about the correctness of having a will to receive in the first place. It's relatively easy to tell the Dinner Lady you want everything, not so easy to believe deeply that it's OK to receive it. So saying, try saying:

'I now relinquish all negative, self-restricting beliefs that tell me it's not OK to get what I want for any reason. It is my duty to humankind to open myself fully now and be a limitlessly vast receptacle for the blessings of the Dinner Lady'

Why don't you?

You probably noticed the word 'accelerating' creep in there, and with good reason.

accelerating the process

While it's true we've become a society of speed freaks, expecting everything we want to happen now, we're still actually going relatively extremely slowly. Consider the fact that the planet supporting your whereas most spiritual teachers will tell you to slow down, I'm telling you to get a move on – with the manifestation that is. your mind, on the other hand, you slow down.

frame as you read this, assuming you're still on Earth, is, as I said, moving along at a brisk 66,000 miles per hour – that's 18 miles per second, or roughly from London to Paris in the time it takes you to read about ten lines of text if you don't mess about – and you realize that no matter how fast you want things, your whole timeframe is relatively exceedingly tortoise-like. So whereas most spiritual teachers will tell you to slow down, I'm telling you to get a move on – with the manifestation that is. It's your mind, on the other hand, that you slow down, by slowing down your breath. That has the effect of making the outside world seem like it's going much faster and will thus allay any restlessness you may be feeling.

This, of course, can be augmented significantly by actually accelerating the rate at which your vision manifests. The way you do it – and I know this will sound very simplistic, but all I can say is it works for me every time – is to either engage in a sincere moment of communion with the Dinner Lady and say, 'Accelerate the process' in the same tone as, 'Cabin crew, doors to manual and cross check' or make affirmations along the lines of,

'I now accelerate the process of manifesting everything I want by a quantum leap'

or,

**'I now accelerate the process of manifesting every-
thing I want exponentially'**

which means exactly the same but may suit your ears
better, or,

**'I now choose my process of manifesting everything
I want to accelerate exponentially'**

and

**'I'm now ready and willing for my process of mani-
festing everything I want to accelerate exponentially
– bring it on!'**

I mean, obviously if you're happy to bumble along and
let things happen in their own good time, then keep it
that way – it's far more enlightened and wise – but if
you're feeling cheeky and fancy a bit of fun with reality, accelerating the process is a good game to play.
I must warn you, however, that as spiritual teachers
go, I'm a very naughty boy, so listen but decide for
yourself – as always.

remember, it's all just theatre

The basic premise that you already have what you
want because you create your own reality, notwith-
standing whether you actually get what you want (or
think you want) or not, doesn't matter when seen from
a large enough perspective. Because from a large
enough perspective – when you take yourself back
and far up enough to see the entire view of your life
from conception to death and then place that in context of lifetime after lifetime – it's all just theatre. The
only difference between it and any Broadway or West
End production is that the blood is real, not fake, and
it all goes on for much longer than two or three hours
– but even that's relative and if you take yourself even
more back and up, one lifetime passes in a trice, as
I'm sure you'll agree when you look back on this one
at the point of death; (a hundred summers when
they're done will seem as short as a single one, goes
the saying).

And while it's nice from time to time to lose yourself in
the drama of it all, you know that's an indulgence, so
be sure to do the occasional reality check and remind
yourself you're sitting in the theatre watching a show,
a trick of the light; there merely to amuse you as you
hurtle round the sun at 66,000 miles per hour. (And

you can play the hero, you can play the fool; you can play the winner, the loser, the victim, the chooser, the lover, the warrior, the volvo-driver, the daredevil, the fashionista, the terrorista, the star.

yes, I'm fully aware I often repeat that information and do so with good reason, as once assimilated it provides an instant key to enlightened perspective, simply because to envision the planet moving that fast through space requires you take yourself back and up far enough to watch it whizzing past, and it's that same perspective you need to appreciate your life and the lives of others as nothing more – or less – than theatre. This view once glimpsed, you are then free to relax into the role and play it for all it's worth. And what is the role?

Well, that's entirely up to you. You can play the hero, you can play the fool, you can play the winner, the loser, the victim, the chooser, the lover, the warrior, the Volvo-driver, the daredevil, the fashionista, the terrorista, the star, the punter, the sovereign, the subject, the object, the creator, the creature, the spoilt child, the wise parent, the guru, the simpleton, the wizard, the holy person, the gangster, the prostitute, the librarian, the driver, the driven, you can play the person shuffling in the queue in the school canteen or you can play truant. And you can switch roles and switch back again as often as you like. You can even play each role in many different ways – play it straight, play it funny, play it tragic, play it melodramatic, play it downtrodden, play it triumphantly, play it up or play it down.

You can take the role wherever you want it to go. You can't control the other actors, nor often the scenery or props, but the way you play it will affect the way they play it and the scenery and props are only scenery and props, but you can take the role wherever you want.

You want to play the role of multibillionaire and to work hard enough learning your lines and getting your entrances and exits slick enough and never wavering from your intention? You can be the multibillionaire. Start acting it now if that's what you want.

You want to play the role of contented savage living in solar-powered isolation in the mountains or jungle, with Celtic patterns tattooed on your biceps and the odd bead in your dreadlocked hair, willing to forgo the dubious luxuries of the grid-powered global electric womb? You can play that too.

If you're really smart, you could combine the two, so at least you could afford a generator for when the solar wasn't working so well-along with a fat 4x4 to transport you off the mountain in a hurry when you got bored and needed a fix of pollution and suicide bombing – you could even have a helicopter.

You want to play mother in the country kitchen, kids playing in the yard, dogs chewing bones and bunnies romping in their hutch, you baking cakes wearing floral frocks? You can – providing you've got the right body parts, of course.

You want to play the party girl ripping up the town, car thieves smashing glass outside, text messages beeping on your phone, you making coffee and wearing a little black number? You can – even if you don't have the right body parts – it's just a matter of a dab of make-up, a bit of a shave or waxing and putting on a dress.

In fact, there's no end to the variations on a theme you can explore, so don't limit the vision. And, as I said, you can switch roles as often and fluidly as you like – there are no rules save the ones you invent. So relax your body, slow down and regulate your breathing and take yourself back and up so you're standing on a planet orbiting a star, say 8.6 light years away – possibily Sirius – from where you can, using a good telescope, get a clear view of your life down here on Earth. Where would you like the theatre of your life to go from here?

Don't slide back into your head when you ask yourself that – remain roughly 8.6 light years distant. Where would you like the theatre of your life to go from here? How would you like it to be in 1008 days from now, or thereabouts? Think about it – no rush – let your

where would you like the
theatre of your life to go
from here?

thoughts drift wherever they feel like going. Perhaps you'll see snippets of scenes, fragments of dialogue, a snatch of a sleeve of a garment, the shine on a shoe, the scent of a perfume, the taste of a drink – just let the images swirl as they want, until … until a picture starts forming and you find yourself fully in the scene complete with dialogue – don't inhibit the process with your rational mind – leave it free to form as it will – and assuming you've conjured a scene you like, look back from there as if scanning back through the three preceding acts of the play that led you to this (projected) point.

Without getting hung up on details, act one is you forming the idea of what you want to achieve. Act two is you going through the process of achieving it and act three is you enjoying it once you've achieved it. But what you're doing here is moving backwards from act three to act one.

So you spend a bit of time rewinding act three, watching yourself enjoying every moment of whatever it is you've manifested, surrounded by loved ones and friends enjoying it with you (or what's the point?) and continue rewinding back into the end of act two, where you see yourself finally hitting the proverbial jackpot, as it relates to whatever your particular vision encompasses, and keep rewinding slowly back, through the series of quantum leaps that led to hitting the proverbial jackpot (and remember jackpot here refers to manifesting everything you want including love, health, peace and, yes, even tweezers), and backwards still, into the end of act one, where you see yourself saying, 'All right, I'm ready and willing – bring it on!' Then still further back until you find yourself here again with me and these words, wondering where you've just been if not here. Well, in fact you've just been the distance between roughly Land's End and John O'Groats or Calais and Marseilles if you prefer that flavour, in terms of the planet's progress through space.

Now all you have to do is walk backwards out of the room so it looks like you're coming in and stand on your head, or whatever you have to do for the action to revert to conventional forward mode as in act one, followed by act two and act three. Which should, if you're awake or just plain lucky, provide you with some practical clues as to which steps to plan on taking next.

The next step is taking those steps, one step at a time, theatrically speaking, that is.

the next step

The next step is like jumping off a cliff. It requires causing your physical person to do something in your world in real time – an action that inevitably involves one or more other people (the Dinner Lady sends it, people deliver it) – perhaps it's a written proposal, a phone call, an email, a text message, a note carried by homing pigeon, courier or butler, or even a meeting in the flesh – an action that will move the story along a notch, however apparently big or small (the action that is, or the notch for that matter), as long as it moves the story along a mimimum of two millimetres or more if possible.

And you take this step without thought of success or failure – you just take it for the sake of taking it – unless of course you don't want to or you're busy doing other things, in which case don't, I wasn't meaning to boss you around. But once you take the next step, the very next day take the step after that one and so on every day until taking steps becomes as second nature and easy as walking.

If you have fear of taking the next step, don't be hard on yourself about it. Fear is natural. Tell yourself,

'It's OK to be afraid'

if you feel too lazy or apathetic to take the next step, stop being such a lazy bastard and take the next step.

then carry on regardless.

If you feel too lazy or apathetic to take the next step, stop being such a lazy bastard and take the next step. If that's hard for you, tell yourself:

'I now get up off my arse and take the next step'

and if that doesn't do the trick, tell yourself:

'I herewith relinquish sloth and take the next step'

then if that starts to resonate, increase the energy by saying:

'I now get up off my arse and take the next step'

and if that doesn't do the trick, tell yourself:

'I herewith relinquish sloth and take the next step'

then if that starts to resonate, increase the energy by saying:

'I now take this next step with courage, confidence and pure aplomb'

and then simply stop messing about and take the step. It gets easier as you get used to doing it enjoy the process and forget about the results until they happen – then enjoy them too.

(obviously). But remember it's all theatre, so ...

don't get attached to the results

Enjoy the theatre of getting what you want, through the hard bits and the easy bits, but don't get attached to thoughts about the results. In other words, enjoy the process and forget about the results until they happen – then enjoy them too. But don't start sucking energy off them before they've happened just to cheer yourself up in a dull moment, as that will weaken their chances of coming through to full manifestation. I'm talking metaphysically again here, so pay attention.

Enjoy every action and action within action associated with each step along the way – I, for example, am enjoying the tactile effect of the keys on my fingertips – I let myself love it – which relaxes my mind, which in turn enables the words to flow through without inter-ruption (from my mind) and furthermore imbues the words and spaces between them with the same enjoyment I feel in my fingers and travelling up through my hands and arms into my shoulders and chest – wait there – I need to have a moment here – a moment of enjoying pure being – thank you, that was nice. Likewise, when you set off to your meeting, interview or whichever event is about to propel you forward on your path, if only the minimum two millimetres, enjoy the tactile feel of the pavement beneath your feet, the air in your lungs, the swing of your arm and the warmth in your palm as you shake hands and you can pretty much guarantee that the result of that meeting, interview or event will be to your liking – if only because you enjoyed yourself being in your body, playing with life like a small child.

So dance with the Dinner Lady, lose yourself in the steps – that is, if you haven't lost yourself already in all these cross-referenced metaphors – hang onto your plate throughout and at the end of the dance you'll get a wonderful big surprise, talking of which …

wonderful big surprises

You create your own what? Reality, aye.

Which explains why, when as soon as you do an affirmation for a wonderful big surprise to occur in your life, it more or less generally always will do just that pretty much there and then, give or take a short time or so.

The only thing is, you can't even begin to try and imagine what kind of surprise it will be, nor in which

I now welcome a wonderful
big surprise to occur in my
life now.

sphere of your life it will come – otherwise it wouldn't be a surprise. In any case, wondering about it draws energy out of it before it's had time to cook properly and you end up with only half an orgasm when it comes through. This is the lucky draw, in other words, so without a moment of self-limiting thought, say,

'Something wonderful, big and surprising happens in my life now'

or,

'I now welcome the occurrence of a wonderful big surprise into my life now'

or words to that effect. Then the trick is to allow yourself to feel the excitement of that without knowing what it will be like and not even trying to guess. Best thing then is to forget all about it until it happens but, when it does, remember to be awake enough to notice and acknowledge it, which may sound obvious and daft but you'd be surprised how easily you can forget to notice and acknowledge a surprise, even when it is wonderful and big.

The value of noticing and ackowledging what you're manifesting lies in the fact that what you focus on grows. Focusing on the blessings that befall you makes your blessings, or at least your enjoyment of them, grow. To remain awake enough to ackowledge the big wonders you manifest to surprise yourself with, it will help you immeasurably to partake of the following ...

developing and maintaining a thankful state

The Tao, if I may be so bold as to attempt to pass comment, includes everything in the entirety of both existence and non-existence, which means everything there is and even everything there isn't. Nothing escapes it. Everything is contained within it, including you and I. Not only that, but everything is interrelated because each unit of being, whether animal, mineral or gas, being contained in the Tao, therefore also contains the Tao (seeing as the Tao is everywhere, both outside and in). So, though in the world of appearances we inhabit, it would seem that all the individual bits and pieces – the planets, asteroids, stars, washing machines, pencils, people, spiders, tweezers even – are discrete beings in their own right, all are, in fact, interrelated, interconnected, interactive parts of the whole.

forget all about your
surprise until it happens,
but when it does, remem-
ber to be awake enough
to notice and acknowledge
it.

Therefore, it would seem as daft for you to say, 'Thank you,' to the Tao as it would for your hand to say 'Thank you' to the rest of your body every time you managed to pick up a cup of tea without spilling it. But while it would seem daft, the rest of your body would actually feel very happy if your hand thought to thank it, and the relationship between the two would improve immeasurably, just as it would between two people in a similar situation. You don't have to thank members of a team you're in for playing a good game but it certainly boosts the levels of bonhomie between you. So yes, it's daft, but so what.

Trying saying it now,

'Thank you, Dinner Lady'

or

'Thank you, Tao'

or simply,

'Thank you myself.'

'Thank you for everything in my life, for all the good bits and even all the bad bits – thank you for all of it – thank you for all of this.'

thank you myself. thank you for everything in my life, for all the good bits and even all the bad bits – thank you for all of it – thank you for all of this.

You'll probably notice an immediate surge of positivity well up in your chest, and that's the important thing – it's not the saying thank you – The Tao, the Dinner Lady, Yourself, doesn't give a damn whether you say thank you or not – it's not interested in protocol – it's the generation of that thankful feeling in the chest that counts; in other words, being in a thankful state and remembering to maintain it, by saying or at least feeling thank you pretty much all the time from now on.

The reason is that a thankful state is a gracious state, or literally a state of grace, hence the word grateful (or *gràcies*, as they say in the region of my trim cubist palace, high on a Catalan hillside).

grace

Grace is that space you enter when you're dancing so smoothly with the Dinner Lady, you both disappear in the blissful flow of it and all there is left is the dance – in other words, you're so out of the way with your usual negativity, fears, doubts and suffering self that the Tao meets with no resistance and is able to generate reality freely in your space. Whenever you find yourself in a space of grace, double rhyming aside,

grace is that space
you enter when you're
dancing so smoothly with
the Dinner Lady, you
both disappear in the
blissful flow of it and all
there is left is the dance.

take it as a sign the manifesting process is intensifying. To access it at will now, use a simple affirmation
like,

'I now choose to enter a state of grace'

or,

'I am in a state of grace now'

or even,

'Let a state of grace descend on me now'

which is strongly recommended as it's a damn fine
space to find yourself in. Try it and you'll see what I
mean. But more to the point, if you wish to intensify
the process of getting what you want – which is
subtly different from accelerating it, in that it implies
packing what manifests and your experience of it
manifesting with more value per cubic centimetre, so
making it more concentrated and therefore possibly
more enjoyable, but that's a matter of taste and mood
– however, if you're in the mood …

intensify the process now

There's nothing better or worse about intensifying the process or not. It's the same difference as taking your chicken hot and spicy or just with lemon and herbs – it's all down to general temperament and what mood you're in at the time. So if you want a quiet time of it for a while, don't intensify the process. But if you're up for a bit of fun with reality, say,

'I choose to intensify the process of manifesting what I want now'

or,

'I choose to let the process of manifesting intensify now'

or simply,

'The process of manifesting what I want is intensifying now'

and what this will do is both concentrate the energy coming back at you from the Dinner Lady and concentrate your experience of it. Every moment will be packed with more energy per cubic measure. If you harbour doubts about your ability to handle it, affirm,

'I now draw on my infinite supply of strength and my
limitless capacity for life to help me handle this
intensification of the process with equipoise and
aplomb.'

But what about luck ...?

what's luck got to do with it?

What's luck? It's the energy of the Universal Dinner
Lady flowing your way expressing itself as an occurrence or series of occurrences that coincide with bits
of what you've been wanting, at which you feel elated,
gratified, satisfied and gleeful.

As mentioned earlier, the Dinner Lady's energy ebbs
and flows in relation to you according to the yin–yang
cycle. Knowing and trusting this removes the unnecessary mystique surrounding luck and helps you stop
feeling so jumpy about its coming and going. And the
less jumpy you are, the more you relax, and the more
you relax, the better you feel and the better you
dance, which makes the Dinner Lady more kindly dis-
posed towards you, which means that she heaps

luck is the energy of the universal dinner lady flow-ing your way, expressing itself as a series of occurences that coincide with bits of what you've been wanting, at which you feel elated, gratified and gleeful.

more on your plate with every incoming wave, which in turn helps you take the opportunity to ease off more every time the wave goes back out, which makes you generally more relaxed, hence more available to your innate wisdom, hence more pleasant to be around, hence more and more attractive to the Dinner Lady, who just wants to give you more and more. You lucky thing.

I'm not even going to say you create your own reality, therefore you create your own luck, because luck isn't something you create, luck is just a description of an incoming wave of stuff you like. But I will say, say,

'I fully accept and trust the cycle of yin and yang to bring me what I need and want in a balanced, orderly fashion now – I enjoy the ebb as much as the flow; I let it come, I let it go – the more I let myself love yin and yang, the more they make things go with a bang. So be it.'

Which is all fine and well, as long as you don't start getting greedy about it, hence the importance of ...

sharing your blessings

This doesn't mean giving it all away, simply sharing what's on your plate, when required by circumstances to do so, in a generous-hearted, warm and kindly way. It may be as simple as giving money each month to the Red Cross, buying dinner for friends who aren't pulling in as much money as you, giving people you do business with slightly more percentage points than they're expecting you to, sharing your home with friends, giving someone your ear when they need to have an outpouring (of words), smiling at and even talking to, as humans, people who work in shops, sharing your joy, sharing your warmth by loving those around you; and I could go on but am in danger of veering into the sickly sweet, so will now desist and allow you to complete or change the list as you wish.

Sharing implies giving of yourself or your resources to someone and not expecting them to return the favour. It is, in fact, the only way to increase your abundance when it starts flowing your way. Which leads us to the subject of ...

other people

Other people – you can't live with them, can't live without them. So what do you do? Well, it all starts with your perception and the way you frame your perception – of other people, that is – both as a general concept and specifically, as in other people *en masse* or certain people in particular – either way, the quality of your intercourse with others is primarily determined by the way you hold the space for others within. In plainer English, if you're willing to find compassion in your heart for others, for their suffering, their pleasure, their sorrow and their joy, if you're willing to see past the flimsy disguises of the butcher, the baker and the candlestick maker to the frightened child in the playground with a brave front within each, and if you're willing to see the best in each, then each, unless a total incorrigible arsehole, will respond likewise.

It's a matter of training yourself to look beyond the illusory divisions between people, tribes, nations, creeds, class, age and gender and accept that we're all family. And you know what families are like – they drive you crazy but you love them. So you look at all your brothers and sisters with your heart gently bleeding for their pain, especialy as you know they

if you're willing to find
compassion in your heart
for others, for their suffering, their pleasure, their
sorrow and their joy, then
they will respond likewise.

could all have things so much easier and more enjoyable if they just relaxed a little more (and even more so if all 6.2 billion of them bought this book – then I could buy a planet of my own and escape all this madness) you look at all your sisters and brothers on the planet and say, 'I love you guys' or simply, 'I love you.'

It's true: that's all there is to setting up a perception of others that will cause them to love you and hence bring you everything you want (Dinner Lady sends, people bring) with a smile on their face, a skip in their step and a song in their heart.

And if you're disciplined enough to look past the surface distortions people display as a result of attempting to protect themselves from the pain of interaction, and focus on the higher qualities within them, it's the higher qualities within that will come to the fore when they deal with you, for what you focus on grows. That's not to suggest you overlook or deny their capacity for sheer roguishness – you remain fully aware of that in case it should creep up from behind and smack you round the back of the head when you're not looking – it's just that you focus your attention, and hence energy, on the finer qualities.

if your motivation is to heal others wherever you go, the results of every encounter will be healthy for everyone concerned.

All this, of course, implies a desire to heal, or make sound, rather than hurt or take advantage of others. If your motivation is to heal others wherever you go, the results of every encounter will be healthy for everyone concerned. It comes back to being compassionate and seeing past the disguise to the goodness within. This is important, because unlike the way it works with the postman (or woman), who is more or less obliged to deliver your letters and parcels, whether he or she likes you or not, the more universal delivery of things sent you by the Dinner Lady can be delayed or blocked altogether if the courier delivering the goods doesn't enjoy being anywhere near you. Conversely, when the courier or couriers like the way they feel around you, delivery times will be sped up considerably.

This is not to suggest you use the act of loving people as a cynical device to get what you want, just that you'll get what you want a hell of a lot easier if you're loving towards others because love instantly lifts you and them above the level of disguises; or you could say it drops you deeper than it, and affords you an opportunity to commune in the moment, rather than simply glance by each other. And you achieve that by entertaining a motivation to heal rather than deal, plunder or tear asunder. So it's not a device but it's a damn good strategy, not just to get your deliveries quicker and in better shape, but also to feel much better about yourself and your standing in relation to your world at large, whether in company at the time or alone. And this implies being aware of your fundamental connection to everyone on the planet, all of us being points of the Tao, as previously mentioned. It also implies accessing the following quality ...

generosity

Generosity describes being in the state of generating, as in generating life, love, warmth, excitement, wealth, entertainment, resources and all the other things people want. It comes with being in a high state of manifestingness, or whatever the word is to describe you when you're manifesting with full force. You can afford to be generous when you're manifesting with intensity. By the same token, you can't afford not to be generous when you're not manifesting much.

This is because the quickest way to stir up the manifesting process is to be generous with others, and this is because whatever energy you emit, in whatever form, does the circuit of the universe picking up friends of similar disposition and, thus, because the be generous and your world will repay that by being ten times more generous back. be mean, on the other hand, and the world is mean to you.

universe is circular, returns to you multiplied. So be generous and your world will repay that by being ten times more generous back. Be mean on the other hand, and the world is mean to you.

So be generous, but don't expect instant results – you have to let the Dinner Lady have her dance – what comes back to you comes back when you need it most and usually not from the people you were generous to initially. It will come back through whichever trusty courier or couriers the Dinner Lady deems most fit to make the delivery. And when this happens, rejoice, because it's like having a ringside seat to watch the magic of existence making its inherent abundance go round (and round). Talking of which …

abundance

So, what do you reckon is the basic nature of this universe: one of scarcity or abundance? Scare city or a bun dance? Which do you reckon? For as you believe, so will it be – you create your own reality.

my Universal Dinner Lady
is voluptuous and abun-
dant with all things nice.
she gives me everything –
no need to ask twice.

You want it scary, you can have it scary. You want to see the Dinner Lady as a scrawny, ornery, mean-spirited devil's daughter, who gives you nothing and begrudges you even that, you can and that's how she'll appear – and furthermore, that's what you'll get – a world of scarcity where getting what you want is like pulling teeth.

But if you want to see it full of everything you want – you and the Dinner Lady having a twirl on the floor, you cupping her buns, her cupping yours, in gyrating rapture and glee – all you have to do is ask and you'll get it. And if you don't believe me, don't believe me, I really don't mind, believe me; but I think you'll find, if you adjust your view to encompass the abundance as opposed to the lack, you'll soon be laughing merrily upon your back. Look, try doing this and see what happens – repeat the following affirmation a few times until it resonates with all the cells in your body and see what happens for yourself over the next few hours, days, weeks and months:

'I am free to manifest whatever I choose –
I have it all to gain and nothing to lose.
And that's no ruse.
My Universal Dinner Lady is voluptuous
and abundant with all things nice.
She gives me everything – no need to ask twice.

She loves to heap the food on my plate,
because the Universal Dinner Lady is my mate.'

(Unless you can come up with a better one, of course.)

will me getting what I want deprive others of getting what they want?

That all depends on whether you create a reality where
the universe's nature is one of scarcity or one of abundance, as already stated, and this means scarcity or
abundance for everyone in it – not just you. So if you
create a reality with a universe whose innate nature is
one of unlimited abundance, and you create it real
enough, that's what you'll get. I mean, we're talking
real magic here, not just superficial conjuring tricks but
full-on professional tricks of the light that affect everyone in your world.

So set about now creating something that works for
everyone in your world, including me – not to your
detriment, not at your expense, far from it – create
something that works for you and works for me and
everyone else too. This involves expanding your vision
out the sides a bit, as well as above and below, behind
and in front, so it encompasses everyone else on the

planet, not just you and your intimates, comrade, sister or brother, in isolation; but every damn person on the planet, even including and probably especially those inclined towards suicide bombing – and see everyone enjoying abundance, each in their own way, enjoying being the key word. Think of the original template and take it item by item if you like – see everyone breathing good air, drinking clean water, eating healthy food in sufficient amounts, with adequate shelter, in good health, with enough money, entertained, at peace, each with their own tweezers and so on. Or if seeing everyone is too big a concept for you, just visualize the people who live next door to the perfect house you're manifesting and see them living likewise in abundance. For one thing, you don't want your dream house situated next to people living in poverty or it will make you feel bad and lower the property value in general and, for another, if you can begin by seeing your neighbours living in abundance, it makes it easier to see their neighbours living in abundance too, and so on, until you cover the whole world with your vision.

And if you think that's far-fetched, naive, idealistic, pie in the sky and altogether stupid, I must confess there are days when I'm feeling rather cynical and despairing of the world myself, when I also think it's stupid to believe you can affect your macroreality to that extent with intent alone. But those are the times I've momentarily forgotten I create my own reality, which you may find hard to believe, the amount I repeat it (you create your own reality), but that's exactly why I do repeat it so often – it's a very easy thing to forget. Which is ironic considering how fundamental it is, but then how many times have you remembered the air around you since you woke up this morning? And that's about as fundamental as it gets.

So I understand your scepticism when it arises and accept it as you should yourself. However, if you spend a bit of time and energy repeating affirmations such as the following, you may be more than surprised by the effects they have on your world, not just you in your world, but everyone else including me, so go on, give it a go …

Say,

'I create my own reality. I create my own microreality as well as my own macroreality. I am creating a world of abundance for everyone to enjoy. The more wealth and abundance I manifest in my world, the more there is for everyone. The more I share my abundance, the more there is for me too. The more abundance I generate, the more abundance I generate for everyone. I am so abundant I could eat myself (and if I had a mouth the size of Canada, the more I share my abundance, the more there is for me too.

I would). Abundance spawns itself. The more abundance I manifest, the more there is (to manifest).'

I don't personally know how this works – I'm not that clever – but it does – that's why there's so much abundance around, if you focus on it. But what about ...

tweezers?

What is this obsession I have with tweezers? You may well ask. In fact, I don't have an obsession with them, but travelling the globe as I do, and meeting many women along the way, as one does, the one single topic of conversation that seems to crop up with unfailing frequency is tweezers.

This is mostly, of course, because of restrictions imposed on their free movement about the planet at airports and suchlike, which seems to cause no end of consternation. In fact, until now, tweezers were mostly taken for granted, it seems, so we can be thankful for the impetus to remember provided by these restrictions and, if we happen to be tweezer manufacturers, thankful for the increase in business we must evidently be enjoying on account of millions of tweezer-light travellers being forced to buy new ones in each country they visit. Personally, I reckon it's a conspiracy between the world's governments and the world's tweezer manufacturers to generate a bit of extra cash and inject fresh energy into the global economy, as I truly can't – and believe me, I've spent hours pondering it – I just can't for the life of me imagine what anyone can do with a pair of tweezers that would enable them to take control of a plane against the crew's wishes. OK, it's true the tweezer bearer could threaten to pluck the captain's eyebrows in a particularly nasty or sadistic fashion, but I doubt there's a pilot in the world worth their salt who would fall for that old trick. So it must be something else, but goodness knows what, so for now, I fear we must dispatch the tweezer mystery to the same filing cabinet as contains the missing sock and biro mystery files.

But what about people in the world's poorer nations, those who can't afford to buy a book like this, those in areas afflicted by AIDS, starvation, drought, corruption, poverty or oppression, for whom tweezers are of no consequence – what use is all this manifesting to them? In other words ...

is manifesting what you want just a game for the world's privileged few?

I was speaking to a young guy recently in Paris; an African, whose brother had just died of AIDS, whose family were living malnourished in abject poverty in Africa, who had to all intents and purposes no chance of surviving, let alone relocating and moving to Paris, where he now drives a delivery van for a clothing company, earning an OK living and managing to send more money home each month to his family than they used to get in a whole year between them. He could hardly even speak any French when he arrived.

I'm not even sure if he was there legally or illegally and don't know if it matters – what matters is he escaped the nightmare and by doing so is helping his dependants – he'd certainly got there the hard way, having trekked many hundreds of miles and risked his life making the crossing over the Straits of Gibraltar, had a horrible time coming up through Spain and had to sneak across the border at the edge of the Pyrenees in the dead of night, which might lead one to believe he may be 'illegal', but I don't work for the immigration service, so it's not my business.

I was just impressed by the light in his eyes, the nobility of character and the sheer force of will that enabled

banish the word struggle
from your attitude and your
vocabulary.

him to make it and believe his Dinner Lady would take care of him whatever. I asked him about his relation-ship with the Dinner Lady, using different terms, and he was effusive in explaining how it was his faith in his version of the Dinner Lady that got him up and out of there and eventually to Paris. He said he saw a picture of Paris when he was a kid and just kept seeing it 'in here' (he pointed to the inside of his forehead), and 'in here', as he tapped the centre of his chest, smiling. So yes, maybe it is just a game for spoilt brats who don't realize how good they've got it, but I don't think so.

and now, a short ditty by the elders of the Hopi Nation, Oraibi, Arizona

We have been telling people this is the Eleventh Hour ...
There is a river flowing now very fast,
It is so great and swift that there are those who will be afraid.
They will try to hold on to the shore,
They will feel they are being torn apart and they
will suffer greatly.
Know the river has a destination.
The elders say we must let go of the shore, and push off
and into the river,
Keep our hearts open, and our heads above water.
See who is there with us and celebrate.

At this time in history, take nothing personally,
Least of all ourselves.
For the moment that we do, our spiritual growth and
journey comes to a halt.
The time of the lone wolf is over, Gather yourselves!
Banish the word struggle from your attitude and
your vocabulary.
All that you do now must be done in a sacred manner
And in celebration.
'We are the ones we've been waiting for ...'

See, comrade, sister or brother? Even the Hopis are saying it and they don't mess around. In 1980 I spent some time with Thomas Benyanka, keeper of the Hopi prophecy, who looked me straight in the eye and said, 'Barefoot, you're absolutely crazy – get outa here!' That's how heavy those guys are.

These are crazy times we're passing through. We're in this together – sisters and brothers holding each other's hands as we crash along in the fast-moving current. Each of us has a responsibility to the rest to manifest something good for everyone now. And even though my tone is far from reverent, you'd be mistaken if you're thinking you were reading a book by a street hawker, a chancer, a mountebank and no good, lowdown son of a gun, rather than a bona fide spiritual teacher of the first order and, even though I really do hate to bring it up, your process of getting what you want is a spiritual affair – a sacred business if you like – and yes, a celebration of life, the Universal Dinner Lady and everything – and you could almost consider it your duty to the rest of us. And talking of duty ...

doing it for the tao

I was just this moment hanging out of a window of my trim cubist *palacio* high on a Catalan hillside, between typing the above title and writing this sentence, and the sky, which is as big a sky as I've ever seen from the ground, is scattered with large clouds of various hues of silver, the peaks of the distant Pyrenees stand glinting proudly, the foothills roll away beneath my window like an undulating shagpile carpet made of pine trees – all different shades of deep green – to my right, the early evening Mediterranean sparkles in a well-mannered manner, and the azure backdrop is lit almost savagely by the setting sun in gold, pink and shocking white light that not even David LaChappelle could match. I almost gasped with the beauty of it all, even though I know the view so well.

Now tell me, if you were the Tao, which on some level you are but, if the local you were the Tao, the undifferentiated absolute at the heart of non-existence and existence before either exists, and you were sitting don't be ashamed of getting what you want and don't be embarrassed – and don't for a moment think it's not spiritual.

there aeon after aeon doing nothing much when, all of a sudden, out of nowhere as it were, like a child suddenly discovering masturbation without knowing why, you started generating a universe, and say that universe happened to be this one and you kept on generating until all the planets, at least the ones in this solar system, were fully formed, and Earth developed life, and you kept on generating yourself in ever increasing myriad forms until you became human beings, and all just so you could experience yourself, your creation from the perpective of yourself as the created – if you were the Tao doing that, tell me, would you rather be looking at some ugly pile of crap or would you prefer to be looking at the one I just described?

That's why the Tao likes to help you get what you want – because it enjoys itself so much more that way – through you. And because there are 6.2 billion of us, and that's without the dolphins and all the other characters the Tao likes to experience itself through in a big way – it gets to enjoy the show through many different eyes at once. So you could say it's almost a duty to the Tao to manifest the best possible picture you can – because that's the nature of showbiz – and remember it's all theatre – especially when you're the Tao.

So don't be ashamed of getting what you want – don't be embarrassed – and don't for a moment think it's not spiritual or the Tao may well get quite angry with you and drop an asteroid on your head – not that it would bother, probably, it would just focus on looking through someone else's eyes instead until you started lightening up and enjoying yourself again. That's how much of a truly sorted ultimate entity the Tao is.

But as I said, at the deepest level you are the Tao, so doing it for the Tao is doing it for yourself. Which is really all a load of old nonsense as is most philosophy, as is most of life in general in fact, seeing as all this is just us keeping ourselves occupied while we hang around waiting to die, which is precisely why it's so important that you …

stop trying to make sense of it all

That's right, there really is no point. Life isn't meant to make sense. It probably isn't meant to do anything at all – it just is. So while you may enjoy analysing and dissecting the supposed ethics of whatever you're doing, while you might like toying with ideas of right and wrong, sensible and silly, spiritual and profane, hold it up as a distinct possibility that your endeavours might be nothing more than human vanity. And if you can get to the point where it doesn't matter to if you can get to the point where it doesn't matter to you either way, when you can entertain the idea of karma, destiny, past and future lives, and entertain them fully while accepting that they may all be nothing but shimmering nonsense, that's when you're dancing the way the Dinner Lady likes.

you either way, when you can entertain the idea of karma, destiny, past and future lives, the day of reckoning, and indeed any of the concepts mentioned so far in this book, and entertain them fully while simultaneously accepting that they may all be nothing but shimmering nonsense, and when that doesn't perturb you one way or the other, that's when you're dancing the way the Dinner Lady likes. And you'll know it because your being will feel light as a feather, you won't have a care in the world, no matter how dire your local conditions, and amazing things will start happening in your life – things you've envisioned and wished for for years.

As soon as you empty yourself of all your opinions about the way life works, and not just all your opinions but the opinions of everyone else in your life – you've made room on your plate, in other words – the Dinner Lady will heap everything you want on it. And for a while you'll rationalize that, perhaps according to the schema in this manifesto, but you'll soon grow tired of that and eventually settle back and enjoy it for what it is, whatever that is. And if that makes no sense at all, it's OK, it wasn't meant to.

One of the forefathers of Taoism, Chuang Tzu, made his name by telling fairly ridiculous stories (not that I can talk) to illustrate the way it is when you've found

287

if you want enlightenment,
don't try and make sense
of it.

enlightenement by following the Tao without trying to make sense of it – this one, for instance, paraphrased in my own words of course:

An old guy, a student of the Tao called Yen Hui (say it to yourself – it's got a great sound) went to visit Confucius one day. Confucius asked him how he was doing and he replied, 'I'm getting better, thank you.'

'How so?' asked Confucius.

'I've forgotten all about being good and doing the right thing,' he replied.

'Well done – but you still haven't found enlightenment.'

A few weeks later, Yen Hui returned. 'I'm getting much better,' he declared.

'How so?' inquired the master.

'I've forgotten all about discipline and rituals.'

'That's good,' replied Confucius, 'but you still aren't enlightened.'

A few weeks later, Yen Hui returned.

'I'm getting much, much better,' he exclaimed.

'How so?' asked Confucius patiently.

'I can sit for hours and forget all about absolutely everything.'

Confucius was surprised. 'What do you mean, you can sit for hours and forget about absolutely everything?'

'I bang my head, arms and legs repeatedly against the wall until I become utterly senseless, to the point where I have no perception and no opinion. I see through appearances and realize that all forms are mere illusions. I stop trying to make sense of anything and like that I become identical with the Tao – that's what I mean.'

Confucius replied, 'If you're the same as the Tao, it means you have no preferences. If you've let go of the physical, it means you have no solidity. That means you've really become enlightened. If you'll allow me, I'd like to be your disciple.'

And they say that's a true story. Crazy but true. Make of it what you will, but if you want enlightenment, don't try and make sense of it at all – and if you're lucky, the sense will make itself known to you – if there is any sense in it, that is. Alright, enough messing about. Let's get serious about this for a while. What do you do when beset by a major attack of the following?

doubt

Funnily enough, I just had one of those. It lasted about two hours and almost floored me – but didn't. The doubt attack, when it occurs, as it does for everyone without exception, when you strip it of all the fizz and bravado doubt attacks come dressed in, as they huff, puff and threaten to blow your house down, consists of a very simple subtext – will I win or will I lose?

And the game goes all the way from the most superficial to the most profound – will I win or lose the game of status, wealth, influence, romance, sex, and ultimately survival? – has everything I've based my life on been just a web of delusion, is my whole life just a lie? – have I just been kidding myself all this time about everything, and I mean everything? Do affirmations really work? Is all the visualizing just so much worthless fantasy? Will I really achieve everything I want? Do I really have the power to manifest anything at all? And on and on, until you stop. For some reason, there does come this point, maybe divinely inspired, maybe the Dinner Lady gently but firmly staying your tumbling head, when you stop fighting off the doubt, relax your body and surrender to it.

'Take me,' you say, 'do your worst,' at which the attack reaches a sudden crescendo, a moment of you seeing absolutely everything about yourself and your life in shocking reverse as if looking at the painting from behind the frame and then it fades away as quickly as it came, maybe after a few seconds, maybe a few hours, sometimes days and occasionally a whole lifetime for some poor souls. But as soon as it does pass, you're right as rain as if nothing has happened and more often than not, feeling more confident, optimistic and chipper than ever. It's like a storm passing through – nothing more, nothing less.

The fact is, if you're here still, you're winning the game – all the rest is just dressing – very desirable dressing at times, without which life would be extremely dull it's true, but dressing nonetheless. That's what you have to strip winning or losing the game back to – the very basic fact of your survival – so congratulations, assuming you didn't die halfway through this sentence – you're winning.

As for the embellishments – the health, wealth, peace, plenty, romance, sex, influence and all the rest of it – simply return calmly and in an orderly manner to the picture yourself as a wobbly doll with a semi-spherical base and no matter how hard you get pushed, no matter how far to one side or another you tilt, you always recover and spring back upright.

original basic template, reignite the visualization, compress and insert it complete with any symbol of your choosing in your loop (carefully, so as not to draw blood), revolve it round the loop a few times and make an affirmation along the lines of:

'I welcome doubt when it attacks me. I relax and surrender and use it to help me grow even stronger and more confident about manifesting everything I want, even if I am feeling a bit all of a wobble.'

Wobbling is fine. Picture yourself as a wobbly doll with a semi-spherical base and no matter how hard you get pushed, no matter how far to one side or another you tilt, you always recover and spring back upright. Indeed, the harder you get pushed, the more force you spring back with.

I must confess, I fear I might have rushed you a bit there – rushed you into the visualization and affirmation before you were quite ready, so I really should add that after a doubt attack passes, it leaves you in a mildly punch-drunk state, almost post-coital in quality, which provides the perfect milieu for a freestyle daydreaming session – at least I found it so just now when my attack passed – and yes, of course I suffer the same nonsense everyone else does on this planet – I may be barefoot, but I'm also human, of that have no doubt (at least). I probably should have mentioned that at the start of the book just in case you were under any illusions I was a perfected being, which I'm sure you weren't, but you never know. And that makes two omissions. But this is no time for self-recrimination (another form of doubt) – enough attack for one day. And talking of days …

what a day for a daydream

Many years ago, I chanced upon one of those books about the secrets of self-made millionaires – I remember, it was one of those plain blue hardbacks from the fifties with gold writing on the spine and dog-eared pages I found on someone's shelf and was riffling through out of boredom more than anything else, at least that's my story and I'm sticking to it – it was mostly a load of Dale Carnegie how to win friends and influence people-style corny old crap, but what jumped out at me was how, according to the author, the one thing all self-made millionaires (but with inflation, let's make them billionaires) had in common was a propensity for unbridled daydreaming for hours on end, almost every day, and had always done so from the time they were mere street urchins, middle-class brats or whatever they'd been before they'd hit the big time.

And while I find it hard to believe that any aspiring billionaire these days could find the time to sit around everyone already knows exactly how to do a strong visualization because all visualization is is daydreaming with a frame round it.

daydreaming, I nonetheless passed this snippet of curious information on to my friend, Jay The Leader, who was visiting the other day – himself a young man used to dealing in hundreds of millions, if not actually managing to pocket the whole lot, but not doing a bad job of it. He laughed and said it's not just self-made billionaires who do that – everyone spends hours daydreaming every day (and night).

So I figured if he's right about that, and he tends to be right about most things, then everyone and certainly anyone reading this book, including, of course, you, comrade, sister or brother, already knows exactly how to do a strong visualization because all visualization is is daydreaming with a frame round it. The frame consists of such devices as the aforementioned compressing the file and giving it a symbol of your choosing as an icon on the desktop of your mind, inserting the file in your loop and revolving it internally to purify and intensify its power to manifest, as well as disciplining your mind to remain positive and thus provide the optimum environment within for the manifestation to germinate. But without a good picture, the frame is just that, an empty frame and nothing more. And while the also aforementioned visualization template is about the most rational scheme known to humans both ancient and modern, it's still only that – a rational scheme – the actual creative part of making a picture that works as a piece of art is all down to you.

And seeing as we're going with the Jay The Leader line here, you already know exactly how to do that. Just let your daydreams run wild, then right before that point when happy daydreaming inevitably turns to anxiety in your belly, as does any sort of projection into the future before long, instead of getting lost in a negative spiral of thoughts about how impossible it would be to actually make your dreams come true, you get Taoist on the situation instead and grab the picture while it's fresh and full of life and whack it in a frame. And talking of being whacked into a frame ...

are you aware that everything you manifest brings with it new responsibilities and if so, are you ready for that?

I'm serious. Did you think you could manifest a whole new life without taking on a whole new raft of responsibilities? If so, think again, comrade, sister or brother. Actually, I have no idea why I'm using that tone with you – maybe it's the responsibility thing – pulling one's socks up and all that. I'm only messing about with you – but not about the responsibilities. Whether it's a relationship, a house, a job, a pile of money or whatever, it requires looking after. Even if you manifest a live-in couple to do the gardening, maintenance, cooking,

if you feel great resistance
to manifesting your vision,
it's because secretly you
just don't want the responsibility that comes with it.

shopping and cleaning in your perfect house, a PA to sort your business, a lawyer to fight your court cases, an accountant to do your books and a full-time couples councillor to keep your relationship or ships on an even keel, you'll still have to take responsibility for paying them and giving them all instructions, however clever a delegator you are.

You know that anyway and it's obvious when pointed out, but you'd be surprised how surprised you can be sometimes when a new raft of responsibilites floats along, bobbing up and down on the waves of your affairs just behind the things you manifest, like a barge full of new tasks towed behind a luxury yacht. You just can't have one without the other.

So it may well be that if you feel great resistance to manifesting your vision, it's because secretly you just don't want the responsibility that comes with it. And that's fine – it just means you'll never get anything – you'll just wind up as one of those people who spend their whole time doing visualizations and affirmations and never getting anywhere – but so what – it's only a game anyway – something you do while you're hanging around waiting to die, and that's the truth.

On the other hand, if you're willing to experiment with reality a bit here and open your mind to the possibility of taking on responsibility in ways that bring you pleasure rather than pain, you'll no doubt, in time, be as astonished with the resulting abundance flowing your way in every possible size and style available, as I am.

And one way you do that is to affirm, by way of making a contract with yourself,

'I am stunned and amazed how easily, effortlessly, enjoyably, swiftly and effectively I discharge all my responsibilites now. I take deep pleasure in responding fully and appropriately to every person or situation requiring my attention. In fact, I enjoy responsibility so much, I just want to take on more and more. The more responsibility I'm willing to take on, the more I'm able to manifest now.'

Take life on as if you're the governor.

But this is really just an extension of taking responsibility for your reality in the first place. And you know why I say that? Because you create your own reality, of course, and you do that by the way you respond to it, in other words by the way you take life on as if you're the governor, along with taking total responsibility for having created it all as it is and being willing to keep taking care of it all, as it morphs its merry way along. So if you're willing to be the governor and accept responsibility for that, you'll have no trouble taking on the whole new raft of responsibilites coming along your way any time now. And I say this because ...

this is magic, baby

See, all this time you've been thinking all you were doing was reading a book, whereas in fact what you've really been doing is magic. Because once you've allowed everything you've read so far into your circuitry, that's it – it's activated and you can't really turn back. And now I am feeling bad, because even though I've given you ample warning from the start about the possible perils and pains of getting what you want and, to be fair, have perhaps been unfair to the positive side of the story by playing down the utter and indescribable pleasure that comes with it, which after all is why you'd have been interested in getting it in the first place; and even though I've kept up that warning tone throughout the book, in my opinion what I haven't done until now is let on about how the text is so liberally sprinkled with hypnotic trigger devices that you wouldn't have stood much of a chance resisting the information even if you'd tried. I really should have told you before now, but I got carried away with the excitement of it all and forgot. And now it's too late to do anything about, which means you're going to

you're going to start getting
what you want now
whether you like it or not.

start getting what you want now whether you like it or not. So forgive me if you wanted to carry on not getting what you wanted – I should have told you, I really should.

But anyway, for now, just act like nothing's happened and carry on as you were – it's only magic after all – something to keep you amused while you bumble along singing a song side by side, which leads me to wondering, so saying, whether you were wondering ...

what happens if everyone in the world gets what they want now?

I haven't got a clue.

But that's the whole point – it's an experiment in human evolution, the outcome of which is totally unpredictable – and that's the fun of it – maybe it will be pure mayhem, though probably not for long because nature, human or otherwise, organizes itself into workable systems. But don't worry about it, if indeed you were worrying about it, as the chances of it happening any time in the next two thousand years at least, are pretty slim – there are just too many people still living with the delusion of being victims, totally unaware they even have a choice in the first place, and you know why? Because you and I have created it that way.

We have created the bogey men (and women) of life because we haven't yet learned to see beyond a reality full of suffering. We're getting glimpses, you and I, comrade, sister or brother, we're getting glimpses but still we find it hard to accept the idea that the human race could actually transcend its present stage of ever more sophisticated monkeys clubbing each other over the head in a constant bid for dominance. And while it may not actually be you and I, *per se*, who go about clubbing for domination, we're still doing a damn good job of delegating that responsibility to all the warmongers, suicide bombers, gangsters, murderers, rapists, tweezer manufacturers and other miscreants of the world, because fundamentally we still don't fully believe it's possible to manifest a world without certain people acting out the dark side.

And I'm not sure we ever could, or whether the intrinsic law of yin and yang, dark and light, hate and love would allow us to even if we were able. But it's worth a try, I reckon – what's there to lose anyway? But visualizing that does not entail seeing no violence, because then all you see is violence – it entails seeing peace. It does not entail seeing no stupidity – it entails seeing wisdom prevail instead. So waste no time and start immediately by picturing an invisible vapour containing wisdom and peace and the good things that come with them, penetrating and permeating the atmosphere until everyone on the entire planet is breathing it deep into their lungs and see it enter their bloodstreams, go immediately to their brains, from brain to heart and heart to belly, until everyone on the planet – every woman, man, girl and boy is filled from head to toe with wisdom and peace.

Just don't grow disheartened or take it too personally when it seems to be taking a hell of a long time to take effect – life's funny that way. In fact, this applies equally to everything you want to manifest.

don't grow disheartened or take it too personally when it all seems to be taking a hell of a long time to take effect – life's funny that way

Well do if it gives you some twisted sense of satisfaction, but it won't help speed up the process at all. Instead use every apparent setback as an opportunity to reinforce feeling OK with things just as they are and being thankful for that – you're the queen or king of no matter what, remember – as this encourages a state of grace and it's exactly that that does accelerate the

picture an invisible vapour
containing wisdom and
peace and the good
things that come with
them, penetrating and
permeating the atmos-
phere until everyone on
the entire planet is breathing it deep into their lungs.

it is precisely at those moments when the process appears to be stuck, that the most profoundly wonderful things are about to be made manifest.

process. The process of manifesting tends to give the appearance of being stuck just before it's about to accelerate and generally only requires you to acquiesce momentarily to the apparent stuckness to trigger profound movement. So you could even experiment with making affirmations to the effect that,

'I now welcome moments of apparent stuckness as a sign the process is about to accelerate'

for example, or,

'It is precisely at these moments when the process appears to be stuck, that the most profoundly wonderful things are about to be made manifest'

and most importantly,

'I no longer need to manifest anything to validate my existence. It's perfectly OK and desirable for me to relax into the role of being nobody with nothing from time to time as long as I do with a happy heart'

which may also require you affirm:

'I choose to have a happy heart and remain cheerful no matter what'

or even,

'These times when the process appears to be stuck trigger great happiness and cheerfulness within.'

In actual fact, it's impossible for the process to be genuinely stuck as this entire universe consists of moving parts – it's all just down to how you're choosing to perceive it. At such times focus on the inherent movement in all existence – the movement of the atoms that comprise this very manifesto you're reading, the movement of blood in your veins, of the clouds in the sky, waves in the sea, and so on, until you're fully aware of movement as an *a priori* quality, for what you focus on grows.

Most of the pain associated with apparent obstruction arises from indulging in the following bogus pastime ...

comparing your self, your life and your process with others

This is a daft thing to do. It's like comparing your leg to your arm in terms of their worth. Yes, you could say the former is longer and thicker at the top than the latter for example, but, as part of a unified whole, each has their part to play – each is just as valid as the other in the general scheme of things. Sometimes your leg seems to be having a more glamorous time of comparing yourself with the minute percentage of people on the planet who are manifesting more than you at this moment is fine if you enjoy the pain of beating yourself up, otherwise there are no benefits whatsoever.

it, sometimes your arm – every dog has its day, so to speak.

Yet however daft it is to compare yourself with others, it won't stop you doing it from time to time because as well as being unfathomably intelligent, humans are, as you well know, given to bouts of extreme daftness on a regular basis. If you do find yourself playing the game of comparisons, at least have the sense to compare yourself with the vast majority of humans on the planet who are actually at this very moment manifesting so much less than you are, it hardly bears thinking about; but if you are going to think about it, be aware that well over 93 per cent of people on this planet are living in abject poverty, all the way from the townships of South Africa or the favellas of Rio to the villages of North Korea or the tunnels of the Manhattan mole people. Comparing yourself with the minute percentage of people on the planet who are manifesting more than you at this moment is fine if you enjoy the pain of beating yourself up, otherwise there are no benefits whatsoever.

Be inspired by the achievements of others, naturally, and always wish them well, as this brings good energy back your way, multiplied, but only indulge in comparison if you enjoy the pain.

This is not a competition. Each of us creates our own reality here but, if you want to compete, compete with yourself. Say:

'Every day, I choose to generate, sustain and manage my reality with more dexterity, grace, adroitness and aplomb than I did the day before because I enjoy my little games.'

But remember to add:

'... and I forgive myself for falling short when I inevitably do from time to time.'

In fact, now I come to mention it ...

forgive yourself for everything now

No matter who you are, no matter how slick you appear, nor even how dextrous and nimble fingered you may be with a pair of tweezers (just for example), you will, from time to time, make what look like mistakes in the way you deal with others. Many times will you stumble on the dance floor of life and occasionally even tread on the Dinner Lady's toes, sometimes even

313

only through forgiveness
can I move on and grow. as
I forgive myself, I forgive
others and others forgive
me.

painfully. I know I do it all the time, and I'm a barefoot doctor – the Barefoot Doctor, even – and that's fine, all par for the course.

What's not so clever, however, is the way you consciously or unconsciously blame yourself for it and use that as a basis for punishing yourself. This form of psychic self-harming is a major blocking factor in terms of manifesting what you want. It causes interference and distortions in your energy field that the Dinner Lady finds quite offputting in fact. So desist from it now and to help yourself do so, use the following device:

Courageously, write a list of every apparent mistake you have ever made all the way back as far as your memory will take you, but leave approximately seven centimetres blank at the start of each written line. When your list is more or less complete, simply insert the words,

'I forgive myself for ...'

and finally,

'I forgive myself for absolutely everything now – no matter how awful. Only through forgiveness can I move on and grow. As I forgive myself, I forgive others and others forgive me.'

And you'll forgive me if we move right along now but we need to make some space for things to fail ...

allowing space for things to fail or morph beyond all recognition

Always give the process space to fail. Nothing depends on you manifesting what you want, even when you could swear the opposite was true. You'll always get what you need for your survival and healthy growth if you remain awake enough to recognize it. Beyond that, everything else you care to manifest is embellishment and decoration. Nothing depends on it even when you think it does – especially at those times, in fact.

If you crowd the Dinner Lady with rigid expectations and stipulations about how you want things to be, she'll get stressed just like anyone else would and will not dance as you'd like her to. So don't crowd the Dinner Lady with your unreasonable demands. Once you've made your desires clear, once you've done your visualization, affirmation or both, set the vision free to manifest as it will. To do otherwise would be like sending an email then chasing it down the phone line telling it which way to go.

it's from being at this very
knife edge between suc-
cess and failure that the
energy to manifest what
you want is derived.

You can struggle your whole life to get rich, for instance, thinking that will make you happy. You may conceivably fail, but find having just as much as you need makes you as happy as a sandboy (or girl) instead. By the same token, always give the process space to succeed. Indeed it's from being at this very knife edge between success and failure that the energy to manifest what you want is derived.

Life is a flimsy business at best, and true safety, security and all the other feelings of wholesomeness you expect to experience when you get what you want actually come from relaxing into the danger, insecurity and other feelings of fragmentedness you're trying to run away from. Security comes from grooving on the insecurity.

And I know I don't need to tell you by now, but you can turn that statement into an affirmation to help you feel secure all the time now, no matter what, simply by rephrasing it as follows, for instance,

'The more I relax into my innate insecurity and allow myself to be thrilled by the sensation of it in my body, the more secure I intrinsically feel.'

Or simply,

the more I relax, the more secure I feel, no matter what's happening around me. security comes from grooving on the insecurity.

'The more I relax, the more secure I feel, no matter what's happening around me.'

In fact ...

it's ok to feel whatever I'm feeling, however nasty

A lot of what you want to manifest, you want to manifest to help you escape certain feelings, such as fear, despair, inadequacy, self-loathing, guilt, claustrophobia, loneliness, hopelessness or sadness. You think if you manifest enough money and status you'll never feel lonely again, but of course you will – maybe even lonelier. You think if you manifest a big enough house you'll never feel inadequate again, but you will. In fact no matter what you manifest, you'll always feel things, both pleasant and unpleasant. The trick is to let yourself feel what you're feeling rather than trying to escape it by getting things.

You may want to look inside at this very moment to discern what you're feeling – then again you may not – but if you do so and notice you're feeling afraid, for instance, rather than do the usual – run away from the fear, distract yourself from it, pretend it isn't there or in any way try and change it – tell yourself instead,

'It's OK to feel afraid.'

Then ask yourself,

'Am I willing to feel afraid and be willing to let go of trying to change it?'

Then answer in the affirmative, as in,

'Yes, I am willing to feel afraid and am willing to let go of trying to change it now.'

And if you remember to relax your body and keep the breath flowing freely, you'll notice the fear evaporate almost instantaneously now. This then frees up the huge amounts of energy required to fight off your feelings in vain, which can now be used instead to fuel the process of manifesting what you want.

Obviously this surrendering technique applies to every painful feeling you experience, not just fear, but equally to every pleasurable feeling too; in fact it can be especially helpful in terms of maintaining the flow of goodness in your life to notice pleasurable feelings as they arise and affirm in similar fashion, for instance,

'It's OK to feel exhilarated.'

'Am I willing to feel exhilarated and be willing to let

go of trying to change it?'

Then answer affirmatively,

'Yes, I am.'

But whichever way you play it ...

you'll never feel fully satisfied (for more than the odd moment)

This is because dissatisfaction is a necessary constituent of the human condition. You could almost say dissatisfaction is the human condition; no matter how much you manifest, no matter how good you get it, it will always be there like a small dog yapping by your feet and nipping your ankles, keeping you on the move, incessantly. That's just the way it is and there's absolutely no point trying to change it by attempting to train yourself to be satisfied. Obviously the training helps, but only to make you more aware of the good things you do have during the odd moment of clear perspective that may befall you every now and then, so at least you feel satisfied when you feel satisfied for a few seconds here and there.

don't be under any illusion about reaching a state of perfection in your life where everything finally fits into place and the work is finally over. It won't ever happen.

The only thing to do is ask yourself,

'Am I willing to feel dissatisfied and not try to change it?'

and then answer,

'Yes, of course I am. How could I be otherwise? I'm human aren't I?'

So don't be under any illusion about reaching a state of perfection in your life where everything finally fits into place and the work is finally over. It won't ever happen ... because ...

the whole thing's just a work in progress

However clever you are at manifesting what you want, however sweet the melody of your existence, or how smooth your transitions between one movement and another along the Great Thoroughfare, your life will always be an unfinished symphony. Wasting time and energy attempting to make it otherwise would be like running round the planet counting every blade of grass without realizing that new blades are constantly growing.

You can never fully complete this task of getting what you want, in other words, so stop trying now and instead accept the transient, incomplete nature of the journey, a stance you can adopt more easily of course by making affirmations such as,

'The more I accept the transient, incomplete nature of getting what I want, the freer I am to enjoy what I have'

enjoy being the key word here. And so saying ...

enjoy it when you get it

This may seem silly. You'd imagine that having spent the years required to manifest your vision, that as it starts bearing fruit it would be second nature to enjoy it, that this would come naturally of itself, but the strange thing is it doesn't. So you have to train yourself to remember to enjoy it by repeating such affirmations as,

'With every breath I take, I remind myself to enjoy what I've got here and now.'

This is fairly crucial because in many ways, relatively speaking, manifesting your vision is the easy bit – maintaining the manifestation once made real is far

more challenging. Hence why empires rise and fall –
they push forth and manifest greatness and splendour
but don't seem able to sustain the energy required to
maintain it and this is because they forget to remind
themselves to enjoy it, and this is true whether it's an
empire of billions of people or an empire of one.
Enjoying it is the key to maintaining it.

is it ever too late to start
the manifesting process?

Only when you're dead. Until then you always have
a choice to optimize or diminish your experience here.
You always have a choice to re-create your reality from
moment to moment. The only limit is your imagination
and the bounds of physical possibility.

is it helpful to share your vision
with others?

That depends fully on your motivation for sharing it
and whom you share it with. If your motivation is
to impress, you'll elicit envy – negative energy that
weakens your vision, especially when sharing the
vision with a person or persons given to cynicism and

you have to train yourself to
remember to enjoy it.

negativity. If, on the other hand, your motivation is to enhance the power of your manifesting process, providing you share the vision with someone who wishes you well, your process can be significantly strengthened, especially if the person or persons you share it with are also practised at following the *wu wei* way. This is the meaning of '... when two or more are gathered in my name ...' In other words, when two or more people share a vision and are both or all aware of the process being a dance with the Dinner Lady, Tao or divine realms, the power of that vision will be exponentially multiplied, hence the reason for group rituals and ceremonies in human society.

when is the best time to do all this visualizing and affirming?

If you observe the internal dialogue in your mind throughout the day, any day, you'll notice a large proportion of it consists in worrying yourself. You worry in the gaps between activities, you worry during those activities, you worry pretty much all the time, in fact, which is fine as long as you find it enjoyable, but if not, use all that worry time to do your visualizations and affirmations instead. In other words, rather than spending those times on a Sunday afternoon, say, when you might have wasted a whole half-hour or

you always have a choice
to re-create your reality
from moment to moment.
the only limit is your
imagination.

more worrying yourself, do something more useful and enjoyable – create the world you want. And gradually allow your positive thoughts and visions to permeate your moment by moment existence pretty much all the time, no matter what else you happen to be doing, from now on till you die. That's the best time to do it – all the time.

so there you have it ...

... everything you want in the palm of your hand, comrade, sister or brother – it's all in your grasp. The internal revolution has begun and there's no way to stop it now. How it will change your life, I haven't an inkling, but change your life it surely will, so be ready – say,

'All change is good, good'

over and over until you're willing to relax enough to believe it could be true.

Ultimately, everything you could ever possibly want, you want because you want to feel peace in your heart and soul, and you want to feel calm in your body – that's obvious. You could, therefore, if wanting to get really Taoist about it, forget absolutely everything you've just read – every thought, visualization

use all your worry time to
do your visualizations and
affirmations instead.

all change is good.

technique and affirmation, every idea, concept and entertaining diversion – and instead simply say with feeling:

'I choose to feel peace in my heart and my soul –
I choose to feel peace in my heart and my soul –
I choose to feel peace in my heart and my soul –
I choose to feel calm in my body –
yeah, yeah –
I choose to feel calm in my body.'

There – I think that just about says it all and now if you'll excuse me …

Happy manifesting,
I love you,

Barefoot Doctor